The Bible Vote

The Bible Vote

Religion and
the New Right

Peggy L. Shriver

The Pilgrim Press
New York

Library of Congress Cataloging in Publication Data

Shriver, Peggy L.
    The Bible vote.

    Includes bibliographical references.
    1. Christianity and politics. 2. Church and social
problems—United States. 3. United States—Moral
conditions. 4. Right and left (political science)
5. United States—Religious and ecclesiastical institutions.
I. Title. II. Title: The Bible vote.
BR115.P7S515   261.8'0973   81-7389
ISBN 0-8298-0465-X   AAACR2

The Pilgrim Press, 132 West 31 Street, New York, New York 10001

The gathering of the information for this book has been possible only because of the alert helpfulness of unnumbered persons who have eagerly assisted the author. They know who they are. They have supplied clippings and documents not in order to have their names listed here, but to further knowledge and understanding of a rapidly unfolding page of history. If through this book that page of history becomes more legible to the reader, they are the anonymous benefactors.

One person, however, is so primary to the author's efforts that only a dedication of this book to him can begin to express the indebtedness and gratitude:

to my husband, Donald W. Shriver, Jr.

with whom I have learned much about politics and religion, But from whom I have joyfully received justice, compassion, and love.

Contents

The Bible Vote

Introduction

> Both [sides in this war] read the same Bible and pray to the same God, and each invokes his aid against the other. It may seem strange that any men should dare to ask a just God's assistance in wringing their bread from the sweat of other men's faces, but let us judge not that we be not judged . . . With malice towards none, with charity for all, with firmness in the right as God gives us to see the right, let us strive on to finish the work we are in, to bind up the nation's wounds, to care for him who shall have borne the battle and for his widow and orphan, to do all which may achieve and cherish a just and lasting peace among ourselves and with all nations.

In the dark shadow of the Civil War Abraham Lincoln uttered these words in his Second Inaugural Address. Although these words in musical form were rejected as embarrassing in 1972 by Richard M. Nixon's Second Inaugural Committee, today—in the aftermath of the Reagan election—they are keenly appropriate. Our nation has undergone another wrenching shift of power, but without bloodshed, and we can rejoice in the triumph of our democratic processes, whether we feel victorious or defeated. "With malice towards none, with charity for all" we must set to work to "achieve and cherish a just and lasting peace among ourselves and with all nations."

This quotation is also uniquely appropriate because of the role that the Bible and the invocation of God has played in the 1980 election. Indeed, both major candidates have supporters who "read the same Bible and pray to the same God, and each invokes his aid against the other." With the exception of the masculine tone of the language, these famous words could have been written for entering the 1980's.

The purpose of this slim volume is a modest one. Given all the clever and profound analyses which accompany our molting season of power, there is no obligation to provide another. The role of religion in politics in this election, however, is worth special attention, including the behavior and response of religious bodies that have not prominently dominated the public scene before. Groups like Moral Majority, Christian Voice, and the Roundtable's

Dallas assembly have not simply sprung up from random spores like mushrooms. They have been a carefully tended harvest. The reactions and responses of diverse religious groups such as "mainline" churches, Roman Catholics, Orthodox, evangelicals, black churches, peace churches, and various ecumenical bodies are still to be harvested. This is a first attempt to gather together the scattered statements and reflections stimulated by the phenomenon of the "religious right."

In the spirit of Lincoln's words this gathering is offered, with the hope that it will further the careful self-assessment, thoughtful debate, and spiritual insight that the relationship between religion and politics merits. St. Paul in his letter to the Romans enjoins Christians not to think of ourselves more highly than we ought to think, but to think with sober judgment, each according to the measure of faith which God has assigned us. Not holding one another in contempt, we all stand before the judgment seat of God, and each shall give account of ourselves to God. Although this book may fail in that noble attempt at humility, it is to this spirit of sober judgment that it aspires.

Who Is Who in the Religious Right?

"The Times, They Are a-Changing"

The vertigo of rapid change has struck our global society, the very fact of its global nature being one of the changes. The United States is not alone in its growing perception that the forces pummeling it are out of control. Technological changes have repercussions, even in the societies that cannot afford to purchase them. Resource shortages imbalance all economies, nuclear threat impoverishes every nation's hopes for the future, and instant communications make noisy neighbors of us all.

In our living rooms we can see Iranian students angrily brandish their fists, impudently aware of their power while holding both Americans and America hostage. Years before these same TV sets burned napalm in our parlors, singeing our consciences as well as Vietnamese children. Americans set aside Vietnam with relief, but the loss of prestige and honor has not been expiated from our subconscious. Some of us harbor unresolved and unexpurgated guilt, while others simmer with the anger of impotence and the outrage of defeat (responding eagerly to Reagan's theme "never again to allow us to fight a war they won't let us win"). Along with this undigested humiliation in the Far East Americans now suffer another one in the Middle East. A huddle of Arabs determines the length of gas lines in the U.S. At the same time, with the toll exacted from our pockets, they purchase land and industries in this country while we watch our dollar diminish in value across the globe.

To some extent, today the United States experiences the humbling role of a "developing nation," which has the terms of trade imposed upon it by other powers. It is hemorrhaging its resources in a negative balance of trade. It is being bought into by foreign investors. And it is sensing impotence with a nuclear power too devastating to use. A recent ad in *The New York Times* makes a similar point in terms of colonialism:

> *How America became a colony again*—and what to do to regain our independence now: Look at it this way: we ship natural resources and food to other nations—and we buy their manufactured goods, like television sets and automobiles. . . . We send our troops abroad in times of war, we cough up the money to rebuild war-torn foreign cities and factories, we let our own factories run down, and our reward is the contempt of the world. . . . Our citizens suffer high unemployment, high inflation, high taxes, and still go out and buy foreign goods. . . . If that isn't being a good colony to the rest of the world, what is? . . . Isn't it time to declare our economic independence again? . . . It will mean flying our Colonial flag again, the one that tells the world, 'Don't Tread on Me.' . . . We did it once before, when we got mad enough.[1]

Anyone who has travelled in many parts of Asia and Africa realizes how overdrawn this image of a "poor helpless U.S." truly is. But the feeling is real, and the loss of economic control also, if indeed that control ever truly existed.

This loss of control is felt not only as a nation, but by individuals and families as well. They worry whether Social Security will exist when it is their turn to collect, or whether the dollars in their pension funds will be worth anything at retirement. People who have been taught thrift along with an ethic of hard work find their savings robbed by inflation and learn that the "smart" thing to do is to spend their savings on goods. They feel cheated and don't know whom to blame. While some people always manage to ride the waves of inflation, and most Americans have kept their heads above water at least until 1980, there is a sense of floundering and many have been pulled under by the undertow of unemployment. Anger and fear search for a culprit.

Change has affected more than our economy and our self-image as Americans. Our daily "life styles" have been drastically revised in recent years, and few people would describe all of it as healthy. A walk in Times Square is evidence of the sordid and seedy aspect of the "new morality," some of which is very old indeed! The loosening of traditional family values has sources so complex that few of us can attempt a thorough analysis. Andrew Kopkind, in *New Times* article "America's New Right,"[2] describes these sources as follows:

> What is breaking up the family are the demands of the system—call it what you will—for women workers at low pay, for routinized work schedules, for education tracked to job slots, for high rates of consumption, for waste and for profit. Scraps of the proceeds of that system have for years been thrown to the most underprivileged members of society in hopes that they will not upset the social applecart; the rest stays in the board rooms at the top.

But he also warns:

> There is a great social upheaval at the heart of America that now finds an expression in the new constellation of traditionalist, individualist and fundamental movements. It feeds the established politicians and practitioners of the Right, and it is well-fed by them. But to disregard its authentic roots in home-town America is to misread the new national mood, and to become its more vulnerable victim.[3]

Some of these home-town Americans who remember the scornfully righteous taunt of embittered and morally outraged youth of the sixties, "Make love, not war!" find it easy to link the perceived military weakness of our nation with a moral decay in our family life. This theme is reiterated by Moral Majority in its call for a militarily strong, flag-waving people who renounce such evils as legalized abortion, pornography, homosexuality, and the deterioration of the family. Jerry Falwell, in his introduction to Richard Viguerie's book, *The New Right: We're Ready to Lead,* says that Viguerie:

> . . . has described the backbone of our country—those citizens who are pro-family, pro-moral, pro-life, and pro-American, who have integrity and believe in hard work, those who pledge allegiance to the flag and proudly sing our national anthem. He has described that group of citizens who love their country and are willing to sacrifice for her. America was built on faith in God, on integrity, and on hard

work. Mr. Viguerie clearly names and points out the actions of those who have not been committed to these principles and have thus led to the weakening and the humiliation of a once great America.[4]

Whether or not one links military weakness and weak sexual morality, there are, in fact, new technologies related to sex and reproduction that introduce new freedoms, challenges to tradition, difficult questions and social dilemmas with which neither the church nor society is prepared to cope. The changing roles of women and men, as motherhood becomes an option for the first time in our cultural history, carry vast implications that traditional morality has not worked through. One is inclined to stand pat with traditional moral teachings or to opt for a private "do your own thing" morality that has the very tenuous religious base of "not harming anyone else."

Just as the technology of sexual revolution poses as many problems as it solves, so science has brought serious problems along with "progress." The word "ecology" epitomizes the new awareness that tampering with nature in order to improve it is more costly and problematic than we once thought in our early adulation of scientific success. Many people are wary of the "technological fix" for the side effects of technology. An anti-technological, even anti-intellectual, backlash has begun in various parts of the world.

A *New York Times* commentator, Flora Lewis, takes note of the surge of fundamentalism in many different societies around the world, reminding us again that this is not an exclusively American phenomenon. She sees profound similarities in China's Red Guard rampage, Ayatollah Khomeini's Islamic disciples, the Orthodox militants of Israel, and America's Moral Majority. She says,

> . . . They all feel they know better than others what is good and bad for society on the basis of revealed or nostalgic values. They are all moved to attempt what they consider purification of what they see as social decay. They all proclaim simple rules defining good and evil to save their worlds from devilish confusion. . . . In one way or another, all of these movements are anti-intellectual, often anti-science, anti-technology. . . . All the movements offer certainties in place of questing doubts, righteousness in place of reason, indignation in place of compassionate effort.[5]

She sees fundamentalism as a search "for lost optimism." If we only repent of our wicked ways, God will bless us again as a nation. This optimism is expressed by Jerry Falwell:

> When people begin to cooperate with what God is doing, you have an unbeatable combination. . . . I am convinced that the real crisis in America is a moral crisis which supersedes our economic, our military, our energy crises. I am convinced that what Solomon said in the Proverbs, thirty-five hundred years ago, is the key to our survival. He said, and I paraphase, living by God's principles promotes a nation to greatness. Violating God's principles brings a nation to shame. The last 20 to 30 years we have suffered shame and of late, international embarrassment because we have been violating God's principles.[6]

It is not too surprising that an evangelical conservatism should flourish in these changing times. One refuge in a time of uncertainty is with people who are most sure of the truth and where they stand. When values are under strain and authorities are not respected, there is comfort among religious people who have an unequivocal source of authority for their lives, who have agreed upon certain key affirmations and uncompromising values. One can be very sympathetic with the basic human need to establish a core of stable truth to sustain one throughout an earthquake of social change. On this point there is little argument. It is the selection of that core of truth and the selection of the sins that need repentance that are most at issue in the current religious debate. This was clearly illuminated by the election of 1980.

Not only the core of faith but democracy itself is being tested by these changes. Tensions over differing values, differing solutions and strategies, differing interest groups, and differing powers cause many people to consider themselves already so outvoted and outmaneuvered that they do not participate at all. As one observer has remarked,

> It is hard to think of a time in Western civilization when the individual has been so subject to society, yet felt so little attached to it; or when society has been forced to govern so much, but with so little authority to govern at all.[7]

The attention of the next few chapters is directed toward a group of people who, largely through the technology of the TV, the computer, and the WATS line, have found a voice in society and are determined to be heard.

"Entrance from Stage Right"

The mood of the nation is a restless one, impatient with things as they are, angry with politicians whose tactics have been inadequate for the depth of the problems. Rapid change breeds change in leadership, shifts in approach, change in direction. Certain astute political activists sensed this as an opportunity. Labelling themselves as the "New Right," they brought together the political philosophy of the ultraconservative "Old Right" and the pragmatic strategies of the liberal "left" which had been effective in bringing liberals into power. Prepared to take over or abandon the Republican Party, the New Right sought power through coalitions of single-issue groups and multi-issue conservative groups, fed by funds raised through a direct mail campaign.

Richard Viguerie, who single-handedly formed a fund-raising empire for conservative clients, is an indispensable figure in the effective emergence of the New Right. In his youth, as the first Executive Secretary of Young Americans for Freedom, Viguerie became disenchanted with old-line conservative political groups. He began to comprehend the potential for large coalitions as he put together the computer technology for various direct-mail fundraising efforts on behalf of groups such as the National Rifle Association, National Right to Work Committee, Citizens for Decent Literature, and senatorial campaigns of Jesse Helms, Strom Thurmond, and John Tower. In 1974 he took on the presidential campaign of George Wallace, and his list-building of conservative clients took a great leap forward.

As long ago as April, 1976, *Sojourners*,[1] an evangelical magazine with strong social consciousness, prepared a major story on the initiative of the evangelical right to "turn America back to God." Their plan was a political agenda of electing "real Christians" with a doctrinaire conservative vision to public office. Richard Viguerie told *Sojourners* that he was looking seriously at the political potential of conservative evangelicals and said he was aware of some discussions for raising money to support such candidates. He said his firm would likely be involved in doing so for at least a few of them.

Almost four years later, in October, 1980, just prior to the election of President Reagan, Richard Viguerie met with a group of religious communications specialists in Washington, D.C., to debate the involvement of fundamentalist evangelicals in politics with Walter E. Fauntroy. At this meeting he named four ultraconservative leaders who had designed the strategy for enlisting evangelicals in politics through the recruitment of electronic evangelists. In addition to himself he named Ed McAteer, Robert J. Billings, and Howard Phillips.

E.E. McAteer is a former national field director for the Conservative Caucus, a farther-right splinter organization from American Conservative Union. He is also the founder and president of the Religious Roundtable (now shortened to "The Roundtable"), which was organized in September, 1979. The Roundtable meets four times a year for two days, bringing together 150 or more Christian leaders to discuss national, political and governmental issues on which they will alert their followers to take action. Viguerie adds,

> The Roundtable aims to reach and activate tens of millions of other conservatives who may play a part when Congress considers legislation affecting abortion, private schools, prayer in schools, sex in the media and a strong national defense.[2]

McAteer is credited, says Viguerie, with recruiting James Robison, the Texas evangelist, who helped assemble the August, 1980 National Affairs Briefing in Dallas, at which Reagan and New Right leaders spoke.

Robert J. Billings, who had been head of the National Christian Action Coalition, formerly the only right-wing religious lobby in Washington, founded Moral Majority and recruited Jerry Falwell, the television evangelist from Lynchburg, Virginia. During the 1980 campaign, Billings left Moral Majority to serve as religion adviser for the Reagan for President campaign.

Howard Phillips, a former aide to Richard Nixon, with the task of dismantling the OEO Poverty Program, founded and is executive director of Conservative Caucus. Howard Phillips joined McAteer, Billings, and Viguerie in a "vision" that evangelicals could be successfully recruited to support conservative causes, including the election of Reagan as president. *Conservative Digest* describes Howard Phillips as having:

> . . . played a key role in bringing together the pro-family movement. Phillips, who is Jewish, has a strong sense of the moral underpinnings of public policy and is a compelling public speaker on the subject.[3]

His address is listed as 7777 Leesburg Pike, Falls Church, Virginia, 22043, the same as The Viguerie Company, which also publishes *Conservative Digest.*

In *The New Right,* Viguerie says that Jerry Falwell

> . . . intends to build a coalition of not only his own religious followers but of Catholics, Jews and Mormons. Significantly, New Right leaders Paul Weyrich, an Eastern Rite Catholic (and director of the Committee for the Survival of a Free Congress), and Howard Phillips, a Jew, worked closely with Falwell in setting up the Moral Majority. The potential of such a coalition is tremendous. There are an estimated 85 million Americans—50 million born-again Protestants, 30 million morally conservative Catholics, 3 million Mormons and 2 million Orthodox and Conservative Jews—with whom to build a pro-family, Bible-believing coalition.[4]

Viguerie's general account of the strategy for enlisting evangelicals in politics was confirmed in *The New York Times* series on the Christian New Right, and the series added some illuminating details as well. Robert Billings, a former public school principal dismayed with government red tape and a philosophy that was coming down from above—humanism, launched out across the country to organize Christian schools where children could be taught untainted. This gave him wide recognition among alienated evangelical Christians and brought him into the acquaintance of Ed McAteer.

McAteer, who had resigned as sales manager for the Southeast after twenty-five years with Colgate Palmolive, had become national field director for the Christian Freedom Foundation, an educational lobby financed by J. Howard Pew of Sun Oil and other free-enterprise espousing businessmen. Over the years he had spent much time visiting and socializing in the conservative churches in his sales territory and the contacts he made there were extremely useful in his new work.

When Billings was president of Hyler-Anderson College, McAteer convinced him to run (unsuccessfully) for Congress in Indiana by showing him a Christian Freedom Foundation filmstrip. During this campaign Billings entered into his friendly relationship with Paul Weyrich who had founded the think tank, Heritage Foundation, with Coors Brewing money. At about the same time, Howard Phillips entered the picture and convinced McAteer to become field director for the Conservative Caucus. In reflection, Weyrich credits Billings and McAteer with putting together the Christian New Right.

> The two of them really had the network between them to reach most of the people that needed to be reached to form these different organizations. It was they who brought Howard Phillips and myself together with the Jerry Falwells, with the James Robisons, with the Charles Stanleys, you know, with all the different people who were doing stuff around the country.[5]

Another coalition of evangelical Christians with strong connections to the New Right is Christian Voice, with headquarters in Pasadena, California. Richard Zone is the executive director and its Policy Committee is composed of persons like Robert Billings (listed from National Christian Action Coalition), Hal Lindsey (author of *The Late Great Planet Earth*), and representatives from such groups as the Pro-Family Coalition, American Christian Cause, Christian Services, and Citizens for Decency Through Law. *Conservative Digest* describes Christian Voice in the following way:

> . . . an important new group whose advisory board includes such New Right congressmen as Sen. Orrin Hatch and Rep. Jim Collins,

lobbies for pro-family causes on Capitol Hill, and issues Christian statesmen awards to members of Congress who score high on the ratings of congressmen.[6]

Christian Voice also operates the Christian Voice Moral Government Fund, which funds a project called "Christians for Reagan," whose Honorary Chairman is George Otis; Vice Chairman, Rev. Richard Zone (also executive director of Christian Voice); Secretary/Treasurer, Gary Jarmin (legislative consultant to Christian Voice and former political activist in Sun Myung Moon funded Freedom Leadership Foundation); and Directors Rev. Robert Grant (President of Christian Voice) and Rev. Donald Sills, a pastor on the Policy Committee of Christian Voice. According to *Newsweek*, Christian Voice

. . . sidestepped IRS strictures on political lobbying by setting up a political action committee (PAC) called the Christian Voice Moral Government Fund. Unlike the other born-again political organizations, Christian Voice has no compunctions about endorsing specific candidates for office.[7]

Although there is not space to quote these communications in their entirety, it is necessary for understanding the full force and tone of Christian Voice to read its self-description. A strong pre-millinarianism and pre-tribulationism flavors this letter to "Dear Brother in Christ":

The challenge facing Christ's Body today is how the remnant of His people may best carry out His admonition to occupy 'til He comes.

The centuries have seen us splinter, debate among ourselves, and even work in opposition to one another in many instances. Still we share in common that only Truth that sets men free indeed, and finally binds them together. And that must be our focus if we are to face the final days victoriously.

Most of us who labor in the vineyards agree that these are the times spoken of by the Prophets of the Word, wherein men's hearts (and even their faith) would fail them for fear. We, the chosen shepherds of the flock in these times, share an awesome responsibility, a special privilege, and an even harder calling than those who have gone before.

America, as a nation and a people, has stood in her brief history as the mightiest (and perhaps the last) great home of the Faith. She is known to the peoples of the world as a 'Christian nation'. It follows naturally that she and her people are the special target of Satan as he seeks to devour the planet and everyone on it. . . .

It is our hope that the Holy Spirit will reveal to you deeper meanings than words can express, and prompt you to ultimately join hands with the more than 1,400 pastors from over 30 denominations who have already stepped forward, for His glory, and the final vindication of His purpose. It is only ourselves who hold back the claiming of the promise.

In a separate sheet entitled "Why Christian Voice" for Ministers and Christian Leaders in America, Christian Voice takes stock of the "progress" we have made for Christ as a "Christian majority in a Christian Democracy." It catalogues the following: prayer banned in public schools, abortion on demand, Christmas celebrations barred from schools and public places, secular humanism and evolution taught in schools instead of creation, homosexuality as an accepted alternative life style, pornography, sexual promiscuity and violence on TV, abuses of liquor and drugs by youth, public schools as a haven for materialist and hedonist philosophies, corrupt elected leaders, government devotion to Secular Humanism with intentions to weaken parental discipline and to control family and church, governmental betrayal of Christian allies in Taiwan or Rhodesia while catering to Godless forces of anti-Christ Communism, unsafe streets, and:

. . . a National Council of Churches, which speaks for 'all' Christians in the halls of our Congress: calls for public sex education of the young; national re-distribution of wealth (à la Karl Marx) and actively supports the World Council of Churches in sending hundreds of thousands of tithing dollars to Marxist guerillas in Africa, whose pre-occupation seems to be the slaughter of Christian missionaries.[8]

This is a fair catalogue of many of the issues to which Christian Voice mobilizes itself and intends to address. Later mailings have included such issues as inflation, taxes, and government regulations. Christian Voice assures its followers:

> These are not political issues—liberal vs. conservative or Democrat vs. Republican. We are not concerned with energy policies, farm subsidies, economic or political theory, etc. These are *moral issues*—good vs. evil, Christ vs. anti-Christ! But these are moral issues that the Secular Humanists *call* political to keep Christians from entering the arena. Christians have been so immobilized that not only have we allowed our Christian nation to be taken to the threshold of total moral bankruptcy, but we are now sitting by while the enemy seeks to dismantle the Church itself.[9]

Involving fundamentalists and the conservative evangelicals in politics is the big new challenge of these groups aspiring to influence the course of the nation politically. Many preachers to whom this letter has been sent are among those the letter describes as:

> . . . ministers who have been conditioned and have conditioned their flocks to remain outside of our national decision-making process. They have been taught that 'politics' is dirty, that their responsibility as Christians is to pray, vote and support the Church.[10]

Furthermore, this letter suggests that these church leaders have misunderstood the First Amendment of the Constitution "which forbids government from involving itself in the matters of the church—but does not say anything about Christians staying out of the affairs of government!"[11] One of the recurring themes of James Robison in his television show "Wake Up, America!" is that Christians must express their faith in the political arena. Jerry Falwell's letters to people who respond to his television shows urge them to become "Faith Partner Crusaders." He says,

> God has led me to wage a Holy War against the moral sins which threaten America. And I'm asking you to help me bring an end to abortion, pornography, homosexuality, socialism, and the breakup of family life. We must put our country back on course. And you know there's not much time left.[12]

A similar point of view is expressed by Christians for Reagan, in a letter signed by Richard Zone:

My friend, our world is being turned upside down and inside out because we Christians have been sitting back and allowing God to be expelled from our schools, allowed our government to promote baby-killing with our tax dollars, supported so-called 'equal rights' for sexual perverts and much, much more. The time is at hand for all of us, who call ourselves Christians, to stand up and say NO to *godless* politicians who have abandoned their faith to gain votes.[13]

To some mainstream Christians who have tried for years to awaken the political responsibility of Christians on a variety of social issues such as world hunger, poverty, racism, and other social ills, it is exciting to hear their words and arguments being uttered on the lips of fundamentalist preachers. Some people are hearing and responding for the first time to a call for responsible Christian citizenship. It is a cause for genuine rejoicing that the duty of Christians to be involved in public decision-making is being recognized and asserted by some groups of Christians who previously denied it as valid Christian activity. To move beyond the debate over *whether* Christians should be involved in our nation's politics into the debate over *how* and on *what issues* and *what positions* is an important step. The viewpoints of these silent Christians ought to be heard.

Not only is there overlapping leadership in these various efforts to activate the religious right, but there is a strong consensus on certain of the issues to be addressed. In line with Jerry Falwell's list of issues quoted above, the Christians for Reagan's National Voter Survey on Moral Leadership (of Christian Voice) surveys the following questions as it solicits funds for Reagan:

1. Do you believe that our public school system should be forced to hire gay teachers as a provision of equal rights? (Yes, No, Undecided)
2. Do you believe your tax dollars should be used to pay for abortions on demand? (Yes, No, Undecided)
3. Do you believe we have a right to demand the prosecution of pornography dealers? (Yes, No, Undecided)
4. Do you believe we have a right to have our school children say prayers in our public schools? (Yes, No, Undecided)[14]

Falwell has expanded his list of issues in a "Christian Bill of Rights" which he promotes through his Old-Time Gospel Hour, seeking signatures to support his formal presentation of this document to the next President of the United States. A close look at these ten amendments shows additions to the issues mentioned:

Christian Bill of Rights

Amendment I	We believe that, from the time of conception within the womb, every human has a scriptural right to life upon this earth. (Ex. 20:13; Psa. 139:13-16)
Amendment II	We believe that every person has the right to pursue any and all scriptural goals that he or she feels are God-directed during that life upon this earth. (Prov. 3:5-6)
Amendment III	We believe that, apart from justified capital punishment, no medical or judicial process should be introduced that would allow the termination of life before its natural or accidental completion. (Psa. 31:15)
Amendment IV	We believe that no traitorous verbal or written attack upon this beloved nation advocating overthrow by force be permitted by any citizen or alien living within this country. (Rom. 13:1-7)
Amendment V	We believe that all students enrolled in public schools should have the right to voluntary prayer and Bible reading. (Josh. 24:15)
Amendment VI	We believe in the right and responsibility to establish and administer private Christian schools without harassment from local, state or federal government. (Deut. 11:18-21)
Amendment VII	We believe in the right to influence secular professions, including the fields of politics, business, law and medicine, in establishing and maintaining moral principles of Scripture. (Prov. 14:34)

Amendment VIII	We believe in the right to expect our national leaders to keep this country morally and militarily strong so that religious freedom and Gospel preaching might continue unhindered. (I Pet. 2:13-17)
Amendment IX	We believe in the right to receive moral support from all local, state, and federal agencies concerning the traditional family unit, a concept that enjoys both scriptural and historical precedence. (Gen. 2:18-25)
Amendment X	We believe in the right of legally-approved religious organizations to maintain their tax-exempt status, this right being based upon the historical and scriptural concept of church and state separation. (Matt. 22:17-21)[15]

Newsweek summarizes the scope of issues that Moral Majority and others in the religious right are trying to mobilize the electorate to support as follows:

> The concerns of born-again politics are defined by Falwell's agenda for the '80's—a pro-family, pro-life, pro-morality platform that, in a triumph of political packaging, turns out to be considerably more 'anti' than 'pro'. Among other things, Moral Majority—and its evangelical allies—are against abortion, ERA, gay rights, sex education, drugs, pornography, SALT II, the Department of Education and defense cuts. They are for free enterprise, a balanced budget, voluntary prayer in the public schools and a secure Israel.[16]

One other way of gauging the importance of this sizeable array of issues upon which the religious right takes a firm position, is to examine the issues forming the basis of the "morality ratings" established by Christian Voice for congressional members. Fourteen roll call votes in the House have been selected as critical moral choices. Without elaborating the technicalities of amendments and motions, the issues are roughly: continued recognition of Taiwan as China's legitimate government; against funds for biological, behavioral and social science research; for voluntary prayer in public schools; for a referendum process by local agencies on regulations by the Education Department; against CETA funds for persons named as law violators; terminating Rhodesian sanctions; protection of tax-exempt status of private, religious schools; against abortion funds; for ensuring that no one is denied access to education on account of racial or sexual quotas; for students attending a school nearest their home; for binding budget levels; a second measure against abortion funds; and for requiring parental consent before dispensing family planning services to minors. Gary Jarmin, Legislative Consultant, says these ratings are not to be interpreted as an assessment of an individual's personal faith, but that these issues are most important to the Christian Voice lobby. The number one legislative priority is support for Rep. Crane's discharge petition on school prayer.

Having examined the genesis of the religious right, the issues it particularly espouses, and the vocal chords of Christian Voice, a further examination of diverse expressions of the religious right is required for a better understanding. There is no better place to start than with Jerry Falwell. Founder of the Thomas Road Baptist Church in 1956 in Lynchburg, Virginia, he now presides over a 17,000 member church and the largest religious broadcasting operation in the country, with an annual budget that increased from $1 million in 1979 to $57 million in 1980. His weekly Old-Time Gospel Hour has an audience estimated as high as 25 million, although Ben Armstrong of the National Religious Broadcasters in which Falwell is an affiliate would caution for a lower figure. He also has founded a Christian academy and Liberty Baptist College, located in the Blue Ridge mountains. Some of his "I Love America" rallies across the country were shown on prime time television, with the eye-catching title, "America Is Too Young to Die."

Something of the mood of those rallies and the television presentations is captured in his appeal letter, October 2, 1980, draped in the American flag and headed in blue and white: "I'M LOOKING FOR FLAG-WAVING AMERICANS!"

Dear Friend,
    I am urgently searching for one million Flag-Waving Americans! And I want them to fly the American Flag in front of their homes or offices on Election Day—November 4th. Why? Because regardless

of who you vote for, I want this nation to know that Christians are proud of their flag! Will you join me as a Flag-Waving American?

You see, what this country needs is Christians like you, who will get tears in their eyes when they see 'Old Glory' unfurled. We've had enough anti-God, anti-American flag burning Americans who are disgracing our stars and stripes. . . . May I send you a Flag Kit? . . .

I'm ashamed of people who are ashamed of the flag—who think being patriotic and pro-American is out of style! Hundreds of thousands of men and women in several wars loved their flag so much that they gave their lives to keep her flying high. Now it's our turn to show we care—that we will work to save our great nation. The Bible says: "If my people, which are called by my name, shall humble themselves, and pray, and seek my face, and turn from their wicked ways, then will I hear from heaven, and will forgive their sin, and will heal their land." (II Chronicles 7:14)

I think you understand what this means! If we as Christians meet the spiritual demands of II Chronicles 7:14, the Church of the living God in America will become what we ought to be. And then God will have reason, not only to heal America, but to also bless her once again.

So won't you please sit down—right now—and write your check for $50 or more to the Old-Time Gospel Hour? . . . Please rush your gift of $50 to me immediately so you will get your Flag Kit before election.

In order to carry out his political goals without endangering the tax-exempt status of the Old-Time Gospel Hour, he broke up Moral Majority into three entities, something like what Christian Voice has done. Moral Majority, Inc., is a tax-exempt lobbying organization for the purpose of influencing legislation on national, state and local levels, and contributions are not tax-deductible. Its membership is roughly 400,000, including 72,000 ministers. Moral Majority Foundation, established to educate ministers and lay people on issues and to conduct voter registration drives, has tax-deductible status. It claims to have registered 3 million new voters. Moral Majority Legal Defense Foundation is also tax-deductible, similar to but counter to the American Civil Liberties Union. Its intent is to battle the "godless, amoral forces of humanism" through the courts. Falwell has also established a national Political Action Committee which endorses and supports candidates. He has been setting up political action committees in every state to raise money to support candidates, with a beginning political treasury of $100,000 each.

One politically shrewd tactic of the political action groups has been to focus their energy and resources on a list of Congressional incumbents whom they considered vulnerable and who, according to the "morality ratings," failed to measure up to their standards. Called by *U.S. News and World Report*[17] a "Christian hit list," they have sought with remarkable success to defeat Senators John Culver, George McGovern, Frank Church, Thomas Eagleton, Birch Bayh, and Donald Stewart.

The motivating fire of Moral Majority can be discerned in Falwell's "Capitol Report," August, 1979:

> For too long now we have witnessed the concerted attack waged by ultraliberals and so-called 'feminists' against the family structure in America. . . .
>
> For too long we have watched pornography, homosexuality and godless humanism corrupt America's families, its schools and its communities.
>
> And when a country becomes sick morally, it becomes sick in every other way. Socialism, which is a first cousin to communism, is taking over the Republic. Today, everything is geared to the state . . . to give-away programs and welfareism . . . to the point where our country is nearly bankrupt. . . .
>
> Now is the time for moral Americans to stand up for what is right and decent in our country—and change what is vile and wrong.

Although Moral Majority's discernment of what is "vile and wrong" in America is concentrated upon pornography, homosexuality, and secular humanism in most of its literature, the January, 1981, issue of Moral Majority Report announced a ten-point program to help the poor, to be headed by black leader Dr. E.V. Hill for a "war on poverty" that emphasizes both the needs of the body and the needs of the spirit. It also reported a meeting of Dr. Falwell with black evangelical leaders in Chicago. The Rev. Hiram Crawford, leader of a coalition in Southside Chicago entitled CROSS—the Coalition Reinforcing Our Social Standing—said that interest in the black community had been stimulated by a visit on

January 8, 1981 from Jerry Falwell, who announced his "war on poverty" at that meeting.

In his promotional brochure of 1980, the purpose of Moral Majority is clear in this "Decade of Destiny":

1. Mobilizing the grass roots of moral Americans into a clear, loud, and effective voice, which will be heard in the halls of Congress, in the White House and in state legislatures across this land.
2. Informing the moral majority of Americans about what is going on behind their backs in Washington. The monthly Moral Majority report will help accomplish this goal.
3. *Lobbying intensively in Congress to defeat left-wing, social welfare bills that would further erode our previous freedoms.*
4. Pushing for positive legislation which will insure a strong, enduring and free America.
5. Helping the moral majority of Americans in local communities to fight pornography, homosexuality, obscene school textbooks, and other burning issues facing each and every one of us.
6. *Recruiting and training moral American men and women to run for political office.*

In light of these goals, the assessment made by *The New York Times* in August, 1980, is not far from the mark:

And it may be, in the 14 months since he founded The Moral Majority, that Mr. Falwell, as a preacher, has done something unprecedented in this nation's political history. In organizing to arouse a particular electorate, to shape the ways it views issues, to register its members to vote, to give it a common language and means of communication, to use it to influence law and policy at state and national levels, to raise funds to support certain candidates and to select and train other candidates for public office, Mr. Falwell has created something very similar to a political party.[18]

This observation is intriguing, especially because the move toward developing a Christian Party of "real Christians" had already been attempted by John Conlan and Bill Bright, along with Bright's various evangelical organizations like Campus Crusade, Christian Embassy, Christian Freedom Foundation, and Third Century Publishers, who, according to Russ Walton of Third

Century have a "vision to rebuild the foundations of the Republic as it was when first founded—a 'Christian Republic'." The congressional defeat of John Conlan indefinitely deferred these plans, and Bill Bright set out to raise a billion dollars for a worldwide evangelistic campaign to preach to every corner of the earth. Interest in politics was not set aside, however, because Bill Bright became one of two co-sponsors of the "Washington for Jesus" rally on April 29, 1980.

This rally, held on the Mall between the Capitol and the Washington monument, also included a pastor's conference, a woman's meeting, a youth rally in RFK Memorial Stadium, delegations to members of Congress, a march along Constitution Avenue, and a sun-up to sun-down program of repentance, fasting and prayer in "the greatest event ever held in the United States for the glory of God." Pat Robertson, president of the Christian Broadcasting Network, and co-sponsor, called it ". . . a once-in-a-lifetime celebration of holy communion in a worship service at the foot of the Washington Monument." A nonprofit organization, "One Nation Under God" was created to run the rally, under the leadership of John Gimenez, chair of its National Steering Committee. He said the reason for the rally was, "Christians share a common concern that the United States has gone off course spiritually and is consequently facing a serious crisis. We believe the spirit of II Chronicles 7:14 is a common ground on which all Christians can stand together and seek God in humility and repentance."[19]

More than a quarter million evangelical Christians gathered for the event. This was, incidentally, far less than the million forecast by its organizers. Nevertheless, this was the second or third largest group ever to assemble on the Mall, estimated Jeffrey Hadden, who found the lack of attention given to this event amazing. Although it was billed as a prayer meeting, Hadden noted, "The political overtones of 'Washington for Jesus' were pretty obvious to almost everyone who paid attention."[20] These ultra-conservative political intentions were clear to many Washington pastors, who obtained in advance a document circulated by "One Nation Under God," entitled "A Christian Declaration." Because of the ensuing criticism from many quarters, such as city council member Jerry

Monroe, most of the city's mainline church pastors, officials of the Council of Churches and Inter-faith Conference, and a pentecostal journalism professor from Howard University, James S. Tinney, the document was withdrawn and labelled as an unofficial draft. Such sentences as these appeared in the document:

> The government has become bloated at the expense of the citizens. The servant has become our master. Freedom and initiative have been throttled by bureaucracy run wild. . . . The truth of God is taken from our schools by action of government, while unbridled sexuality, humanism, and satanism are taught at public expense.

In reaction to the draft's position and tone, the Washington Interreligious Staff Council issued a joint statement of "explicit disagreement."[21]

Controversy has seldom held back press coverage. But in this instance several factors combined to dilute the exposure this gathering received. For one, as much attention was directed to the protestors of this event as to the event itself. For another, many other important stories were also on public view: the appointment of Senator Muskie as Secretary of State following the resignation of Cyrus Vance, and the continuing preoccupation of the press with the Iranian hostage issue. Still, some first hand accounts were published such as the following:

> 'I love America and I love Jesus' was shouted repeatedly—antiphonally by speakers and the crowd. . . . Over and over speakers proclaimed, 'God loves America!' . . . There was a desperate desire in the faces of the people, a yearning in the words of the speakers, a plaintive longing in the lyrics of the songs to believe in the return of something that has never been—America as a 'bible-believing, born-again Christian nation.'[22]

There were other less dispassionate accounts as well. One religiously sensitive and sympathetic account, though firmly critical at certain important points, was provided in a *Harper's* article by Dick Dabney, himself an evangelical. His attendance at the event was informed by prior interviews and a visit to Pat Robertson's headquarters at Christian Broadcasting Network near Virginia Beach, Virginia. He observed:

> You feel (excitement) thick all around you, people raising hands to God and praying for Him to spare the country, and singing the old, soul-stirring hymns, not through a little speaker on a TV set, but from all around you. And as in a good rock concert, you know that no television set could ever convey the way this thing felt, with all the power around you exceeding the wattage being put forth up there on the platform, where a succession of born-again superstars were waiting to come on and give sermons. . . .
>
> Just maybe, I thought, Robertson means what he says about the repentance and is up there at this moment repenting of the way he wreaks those infernal Kingdom Principles on poor and helpless people. And if that was the case, I thought, then a whole lot of other things could be possible, because a Pat Robertson purged of the itch for corporate expansion, self-righteousness, and the lust for political power really would be formidable. With his great ability, he might just trigger that third great awakening that so many Christians were calling for but that had not come close to happening yet. But I understate it by saying 'just maybe', because the power of the experience, and this overwhelming feeling that these people were good whether their leaders were or not, washed over me, and I went away from there feeling that it probably had happened, Robertson's repentance.[23]

Whether or not the indictment by Washington's religious leaders and articles like the one just quoted had an impact upon Robertson, only he can truly say. But since that rally he has clearly become less identified with those who moved on to establish the Dallas National Affairs Briefing. Indeed, the September 15, 1980 *Newsweek* quotes Pat Robertson as saying, "God isn't a right-winger or a left-winger. The evangelists stand in danger of being used and manipulated." It further notes Robertson as arguing that "active partisan politics" is the wrong path for true evangelicals. "There's a better way; fasting and praying . . . appealing, in essence, to a higher power." This is in contrast to *Christianity Today's* write-up of a year earlier:

> The son of a former U.S. Senator from Virginia, Robertson has openly backed conservative Christian candidates in that state, and he

has invited several conservative congressmen as guests on the "700 Club." The program is viewed by millions on 150 TV stations and about 3,000 cable systems.

Robertson has publicly questioned President Carter's competence, warned against the excessive influence of liberals in public policy, and suggested that the American government is really under the control of a leftist elite. Conservative Catholics and Protestants need to unite to rescue America, he says. Together, he wrote recently, we have enough votes to run the country.[24]

U.S. News and World Report also had reported in 1979 that Robertson sends a monthly newsletter to interested callers, and it contains the evangelist's interpretations of current events, free from the constraints of broadcasting's fairness doctrine.

In foreign affairs, his persistent theme is that the world is moving, in fulfillment of the Bible's Judgment Day prophecies, toward a war, probably fought with nuclear weapons, over the Middle Eastern Holy Land.

'When the smoke clears,' Robertson writes, 'Soviet Russia will be reduced to a fourth-rate power and Israel will be the wonder of the world. That is what the Bible tells us will happen, and it will happen!' . . . 'Unless Christians desire a nation and a world reordered to the humanistic/atheistic/hedonistic model, it is absolutely vital that we take control of the United States government away from the Trilateral Commission and the Council on Foreign Relations.'[25]

In the summer of 1980, however, Dick Dabney's article reported Robertson to have maintained his expectation of the catastrophic End Times to be near, belief that the Trilateral Commission wants to take over the world and destroy democracy and Christianity, and that "In the event of a major breakdown, the country might turn to us." With his goals apparently unchanged, he may simply be looking for different companions in evangelical circles for carrying them out.

Less well-known than the television personalities and their related organizations is a group called Intercessors for America (IFA), founded by John G. Talcott, Jr., director of Ocean Spray Cranberries. A similar group, the Greater Miami Prayer Chain, was organized by Bill Bright of Campus Crusade, along with his other previously discussed religious/political connections. Intercessors for America is a tax-exempt prayer chain organized by means of a newsletter that "focuses on subjects requiring national attention through prayer such as pornography and fiscal integrity." Calling Christians to united intercessory prayer and fasting for America, IFA provides background information on the issues with a clear sense of the Christian position. For example, when encouraging intercessors to pray against ERA, it supplied a two-page anti-ERA tract using much of Phyllis Schlafly's material, including her report on the International Women's Year Conference. It urged intercessors to "pray too that the press, our legislators, and our President will not be persuaded by this conference." Other issues include the Panama Canal treaties, national defense (vs. SALT II), and gay rights.

In addition to prayer and fasting, intercessors are called upon to "salt" their communities; a practical suggestion for "salting" is to write government leaders and newspaper editors or to address local church and community groups on these issues. "Putting feet to their prayers" is the praise given to persons who write their viewpoints to television stations, Congress, and the state legislatures. Prayer chains are often accomplished by telephone calls as well. IFA reported in 1977 that prayer was instrumental in the defeat of the "Gay Rights Bill" in Minnesota when, "In less than twenty-four hours, 100 prayer chains were contacted and hundreds of phone calls were made to key legislators."[26]

While few American citizens are aware of such groups as Intercessors for America, most of them received some word about the Dallas National Affairs Briefing, sponsored by the Christian Roundtable. It was designed as a media event, with Reagan as a key speaker. Over 400 press people responded, along with all the major radio and television networks, and over a dozen foreign correspondents. Jeffrey Hadden, a sociologist who attended, noted somewhat ironically that this event was really not very important as an instrument for direct mobilization of born-again politicians. He wrote that only about 250 people attended a quickly scheduled post-Briefing session on the nuts and bolts of getting organized. He also reported that no more than 2,500 born-again pastors had showed up for the Briefing in the first place. This was quickly remedied by putting out word that the meetings were open to the public for a modest fee. Quickly the prime time events were filled with the addition of local lay Christians. Hadden says with a touch of mockery,

> Apparently no one told all those Eastern Establishment press persons that there are a dozen circuit riding evangelists who could fill the largest arena in Texas at the drop of a hat.[27]

Although Reunion Arena was crowded with exhibits by organizations such as Christian Voice, Pro-Family Forum, National Prayer Campaign, Eagle Forum, Right to Life Commission, Fund to Restore an Educated Electorate, and the Institute for Christian Economics, Hadden claims that many journalists left with a more tolerant and complex view of these people than when they arrived, less certain that this was the dawning of a fascist political party in America. Like Bill Moyers, who spoke of the Dallas gathering as "my people, good people," Hadden says, "Basically these are good people who have in common their evangelical faith and the fact that they are fighting mad about the way things are going in America." One of the few remarks of concern for the poor and minorities that appears in this systematic sifting of statements from the religious right was expressed by James Robison, who spoke eloquently about the poor and minorities as political pawns and urged his audience:

> Quit criticizing the system and the welfare programs and get out there in the ditch with people that need help and get dirty with them until you get them out. You've got no business applauding until you're willing to get in the ditch with people.[28]

It was at this same event, however, that Dr. Bailey Smith, president of the Southern Baptist Convention, offended and shocked many people with his words:

> It is interesting at great political rallies how you have a Protestant to pray, a Catholic to pray, and then you have a Jew to pray. With all due respect to those dear people, my friends, God Almighty does not hear the prayer of a Jew.

For how in the world can God hear the prayer of a Jew, or how in the world can God hear the prayer of a man who says that Jesus Christ is not the true Messiah? That is blasphemy. It may be politically expedient, but no one can pray unless he prays through the name of Jesus Christ.[29]

While taking note of who was present in Dallas (and the speakers list is an impressive "Social Register" of the New Right: Paul Weyrich, Phyllis Schlafly, Ed Rowe, Adrian Rogers, Howard Phillips, Ed McAteer, Connie Marshner, Tim LaHaye, Sen. Jesse Helms, Rep. Phillip Crane, Govs. Clements and Connally, Sen. Bill Armstrong, Brig. Gen. Albion Knight, Major Gen. George Keegan, Rep. Guy Vander Jagt, television preachers Jerry Falwell, Pat Robertson, and James Robison, and candidate Ronald Reagan), one is often less alert to persons who were *not* there. Billy Graham carefully kept his distance from this assembly. Jim Bakker of PTL, a religious TV network like Christian Broadcasting Network, which also has developed assorted additional ministries such as the plush multi-million dollar Fort Heritage Retreat Center, was not involved. Absent, at least from any records of the event, were such figures as Oral Roberts, Rex Humbard, and Robert Schuller. In general, the National Association of Evangelicals leadership, with headquarters in Wheaton, has taken a very cautious stand toward the "evangelical right," and comments from this middle-ground of evangelicalism appear in the commentary section of this book.

Before moving on to that commentary, however, it is useful to place these various groups on the "Pro-Family Tree," because concern for issues broadly defined as affecting the family is the "glue" that holds these various groups together. In addition, an analysis of the public to which this Pro-Family Movement appeals, no matter how hazardous the effort, may contain some insight.

The Pro-Family Tree

It is evident that these highlighted issues of the religious right cluster around a core of concern which the New Right labels

"Pro-Family." The *Conservative Digest*[1] devoted its May/June 1980 issue to a special report on the "Pro-Family Movement." **Congressional leaders** it listed are: Sen. Jake Garn, Sen. Orrin Hatch, Sen. Jesse Helms, Sen. Gordon Humphrey, Sen. Paul Laxalt, and Representatives John Ashbrook, Bob Bauman, Phil Crane, Bob Dornan, Henry Hyde, Jim Jeffries, Larry McDonald, and Bob Walker. Organizations that compose the **"Washington Connection"** are Citizens for Educational Freedom (Bob Baldwin), National Christian Action Coalition (Bill Billings), Moral Majority (formerly Robert Billings), Free Congress Foundation (Connie Mashner), Conservative Caucus (Howard Phillips), and American Legislative Exchange Council (Kathy Teague).

Pro-Family organizations listed by *Conservative Digest* are: Catholic League for Religious and Civil Rights (Fr. Blum), Pro-Family Forum (Lottie Beth Hobbs), Life Advocates (Margaret Hotze), Citizens for Constructive Education (June Larson), Stop-ERA and Eagle Forum (Phyllis Schlafly), White House Conference on Families Review Board (Rosemary Thomson), and Leadership Foundation (Martha Rountree). Also mentioned are the following publications: *Right Woman* and *Register Report* (ed. JoAnn Gasper), *Family Protection Report* (Marshner), *Moral Majority Report* (Harry Covert, ed.), *The Life Advocate* (Hotze), *Christian's Political Action Manual* and *Family Issues Voting Index* (Bill Billings), and *Christian Inquirer* (ed., Ron Marr).

Another branch of this Pro-Family Tree is listed by *Conservative Digest* as the **"Evangelicals."** They are: National Organization to Involve Concerned Electorate (Wayne Allen), Intercessors for America (John Beckett), Moral Majority (Jerry Falwell), Concerned Women for America (Beverly LaHaye and husband Tim), Religious Roundtable (Ed McAteer), Chriswell Institute of Biblical Studies (Paige Patterson), Christian Broadcasting Network's "700 Club" (Pat Robertson), Christian Coalition for Legislative Action (Jim Wright), Esther Action Council in United Methodist Church (LaNeil Wright), and Christian Voice (Richard Zone). The following evangelists and pastors are also mentioned: Richard Hogue of Oklahoma, James Dobson (California radio psychologist), Jerry Prevo of Alaska, Ross Rhoads of Charlotte, N.C., Adrian Rogers who was president of the Southern Baptist

Convention, Charles F. Stanley of Atlanta, and James Robison of Texas and the Dallas National Briefing.

Another major branch of the Pro-Family Tree is the **Pro-Life Movement.** Listed as key organizations and leaders of pro-life are: Life Amendment Political Action Committee (Paul Brown), American Life Lobby (Judie Brown), U.S. Coalition for Life (Randy Engel), and National Pro-Life Political Action Committee (Fr. Charles Fiore, chair; Peter B. Gemma, national director). Mary Jane Tobin and Ellen McCormack are recognized for seeking office on a right to life agenda, and Fran Watson is named for her leadership of both the New York State Right to Life Party and the Citizens for Judicial Restraint.

Many of the organizations and leaders above have a special interest in **education** issues, but to the following, these issues are central: Norma and Mel Gabler of Educational Research, Inc.; Onalee McGraw of Heritage Foundation and The Coalition for Children; and Jack Clayton of American Association of Christian Schools.

McGraw strongly opposes federal daycare centers and the Gablers are well known for monitoring school textbooks, (written about in *Textbooks on Trial*). At the Anaheim Fifteenth Anniversary Creation Convention, which sought to introduce scientific creationism into school science books, the Gablers conducted a textbook workshop. The Creation Science Research Center was formed to combat the "unconstitutionality of the exclusive teaching of evolution in the public schools," but its newsletter, *Creation Science Report,* also opposed ERA, sex education, abortion, and Planned Parenthood, among other issues.

Anti-pornography as a branch of the Pro-Family Movement is represented most specifically by Morality in Media (Fr. Morton Hill) and the National Federation for Decency (Donald Wildmon), though it is clearly an issue supported by many other groups. Also, special concern for **anti-homosexual** activity is accorded to Anita Bryant's "Save Our Children" crusade and to Fletcher Brothers of Rochester, N.Y., who wages his anti-homosexual campaign on a six-station radio program which is expanding across the country.

The complex network of organizations and leaders that compose the Pro-Family Movement has been formed into a coalition which meets weekly in Washington, D.C. It's called the *Library Court,* after the street where its original meetingplace was located in Committee on Survival of a Free Congress offices. It does not see itself as a subset of the conservative movement. A participant observed in *Conservative Digest* that "the New Right influences the pro-family movement only to the extent that it shares the movement's God-centered views and that the movement needs the New Right's technical guidance." However, Paul Weyrich was active in forming the group and is a member, and Connie Marshner is active in the Committee for Survival of a Free Congress.

Connaught (Connie) Marshner, who chairs the Library Court as well as being director of the Family Policy Division of the Free Congress Foundation, has assisted Sen. Paul Laxalt in drafting the centerpiece of Pro-Family legislation, the Family Protection Act (S. 1808 and H.R. 6028) as "the best strategic tool available to the pro-family movement." It is an omnibus bill that bears very close reading, and a summary of it is appended to this book (p.150). Although it is described in terms of family protection, it covers many education issues, welfare, regulation of religious institutions, tax revisions, abortion, child abuse, school desegregation, homosexual rights, and food stamp eligibility. Many of these may not come readily to mind as involved in such an act. Some of its provisions would receive hearty endorsement from many quarters in the populace, including many liberals, but there are other provisions which require much public debate.

Right Face

Terms like "evangelical," "fundamentalist," "conservative," "New Right," "Old Right," "Neoconservative," "Extremist," "religious right," and their counterparts to the "left" are as slippery as jello to define, and the harder one looks at them the more they seem to melt and blur. Yet we use these terms because we know that, despite their elusiveness, there is some reality being addressed. Without at least self-identifying name tags we have difficulty speaking to and about one another. While not attempting to put fences around any of these terms, this book works chiefly with self-chosen labels, but even then some words of caution are needed. Self-perception, for example, has its own limitations. Few persons would label themselves "extremists." The definition used for self-identification may be as quixotic and vague as an individual chooses, so that the label becomes meaningless to others with different definitions. And a terminology with very positive meaning to one individual is invidious to another. Persons may therefore choose to share the same label but be really quite different.

It is a delicate exercise, therefore, to attempt in any way to describe the "religious right," except by the positions on issues they have taken and the groups with whom they have chosen to associate themselves. Thus far, this book has attempted to respect that cautious approach. In the process, however, some concern for distortion and neglect of certain facts emerges.

An example of this concern is the treatment by the public press of "evangelicals," with an estimate of numbers that slides from a low of 30 million (Gallup's tight definitional estimate) to as high as 85 million. The problem is not only the stringency of definition, but an assumption that—if they are evangelicals—they are a vast pool into which the "religious right" can continue to dip. Evangelicals are *not* of one political stripe, as even a cursory glance at the history of evangelicalism in this country would show. David O. Moberg reminds us in his essay in *The Evangelicals:*

> Since evangelicals come from a broad range of theological, denominational, historical, educational, cultural, ethnic, and other backgrounds, it is no wonder that they do not comprise a homogeneous segment of the population on anything other than the central tenets of faith which give them a distinctive identity in our pluralistic society. Even the faith position may be variously interpreted on the levels of implications for action, internalized subtleties of meaning, and depth of convictions.[1] [The wide range of evangelical perspectives on political, philosophical, scientific, social action, and even theological issues is documented in other chapters of this book as well as in the implicit and explicit discussions of numerous important interpretative and exhortative works.]

Gallup's poll on the 30 million evangelicals he defines as comprising one fifth of the adult population were seen in September to be 52% for Carter, 31% for Reagan, and 6% for Anderson, at a time when the general population was split 39%-38%-13%. His survey offered a very mixed picture, with born-again Christians favoring ERA—but by a slimmer majority than other Americans—and at the same time strongly favoring required prayer in public schools.[2] Timothy L. Smith, who is the author of *Revivalism and Social Reform* and director of a research project on "The American Evangelical Mosaic," calls to our mind the evangelicals who are the majority in the historic peace churches. They are: Brethren, Mennonites, and Quakers, who do not countenance militarism; the Southern Baptist Convention's thirteen million whose heritage treasures the separation of church and state and whose goal is a kingdom of love; the Churches of Christ in America with over 2.5 million evangelicals who are not caught up in the doomsday biblical prophesy that infuses much television preaching; the black evangelicals who may well constitute a third of all evangelicals in this country, but who are only tokenly represented in "I Love America" rallies; and the Salvation Army, the Nazarenes, and some radical Wesleyan groups that are devoted to people trapped by racism or poverty. Smith says that this broad community of evangelicals deplores Falwell's efforts to build a power bloc in its name and marvels that the news media countenance his claim to speak for them.[3]

Smith's description of evangelical diversity is underscored by several noted evangelical leaders. Robert P. Dugan, Jr., executive director of the National Association of Evangelicals said to a Wheaton forum, "There is no evangelical bloc. There is no common political philosophy uniting evangelicals. Evangelicals won't determine the outcome of the election but they may think they have if Reagan is elected." Billy Graham, also addressing a Wheaton group, said, "I heard a preacher on TV say that 'we can elect any president we want.' But we can't. Those involved in this political movement are a very small segment of evangelicals." Evangelical leader Stan Mooneyham said, "Surely, Jesus' prayer for his disciples and for us that we might all be one did not necessarily mean pulling the same voting machine lever."[4]

The diversity among evangelicals in religious practice and in theological emphasis is also seldom noted in the press. Pentecostals emphasize the importance of spiritual empowerment and conversion and tend to resist political involvement or identification with social causes. Largely poor and white, their separation by class from most liberal churches has contributed to their lack of involvement in anti-liberal and anti-humanist attacks. Among the pentecostals are Jimmy Swaggart, Oral Roberts, Jim Bakker, and to some extent Pat Robertson, although he has become politically involved. Fundamentalists like Jerry Falwell, however, and many Southern Baptists, are critical of pentecostals as well as of liberals and "secular humanists." They have had forays into politics and morality in the past, such as the promotion of Prohibition. Black fundamentalist Baptists have long had a rigorous political activism.

Professor Gerald Sheppard of Union Theological Seminary puts evangelicalism into some historical perspective in remarks he made during a symposium sponsored by Reformed Judaism in New York City, January 19, 1981:

> Historically, evangelicalism arose out of a loss of social status by fundamentalists in the 1920s. William Jennings Bryan, one of the most prominent fundamentalists of his time, ran for president of the United States. But after the repeal of Prohibition, fundamentalists were forced out of the universities, and out of almost every major social position, becoming an embittered group of misplaced middle Americans. In the 1940s, a respectable evangelicalism emerged around the creation of such groups as the National Association of Evangelicals, seminaries like Fuller, the success of the Billy Graham Crusades and magazines like *Christianity Today*. Such groups represent a moderate evangelicalism which wants to overcome the social naiveté and rigidity of the earlier fundamentalists.
>
> Evangelicalism is a closed social system, a movement with its own presses, its own seminaries, and its own Bible colleges or Christian liberal arts colleges. It is a self-ghettoizing American social movement of the white middle class. It does not have prominent participation by blacks or Hispanics. . . . People like Jerry Falwell and those he appeals to, however, are usually without college backgrounds, yet they establish Christian colleges and universities as alternative institutions to the worldly ones which they didn't attend

and which they don't want their children to attend. They are lower middle class white Americans who feel that they have lost control and power. Falwell is successful because he gives them a voice, a new sense of social esteem.[5]

Less sure of this characterization of Falwell's following is Gerald Strober of American Friends of Tel Aviv University and biographer of Jerry Falwell, who commented on that same occasion:

> His constituency, the people who wait for hours to shake his hand after a meeting, are middle class and suburban oriented. They own their own homes, have a couple of credit cards, are fairly modern in their business and professional life, are well educated, and might even fit into Manhattan cocktail parties if they didn't dislike the idea of having alcoholic beverages.[6]

A doctoral dissertation by John Stephen Hendricks utilizes data from the Survey Research Center and the National Opinion Research Center to disclose some unexpected shifts concerning fundamentalists in the United States.[7] According to Hendricks, there has been, during the prosperity of the late fifties and sixties, a significant rise in the socio-economic and educational status of fundamentalists. There is a growing middle class conservative theological and political group which has not apparently followed the previously well-documented shift to mainline denominations as fortunes and educational opportunities have expanded. Although this does not necessarily mean increased numbers, it does indicate increasing resources and skills in the religious right.

Election returns showed that the black population was not persuaded to the Reagan platform, or to the New Right itself. Other minority groups, such as Hispanics and Asians, are also visibly absent from religious right gatherings and leadership. White European ethnic groups, particularly those who are still self-con-sciously "Americanized," are much more likely than racial minorities to be attracted to the New Right and its emphasis upon patriotism. Many disaffected ghetto blacks are not easily drawn toward patriotism, nor toward political participation, and they suspect that conservative economists care little about black unemployment. Charles V. Hamilton of Columbia University says that it would be a mistake to conclude that black middle-class attitudes on economic issues are similar to those of disaffected middle-class whites, because they are deeply tied to the public sector economy. While 17% of the population as a whole work for the government, 67% of all black professionals and managers work for the government. Black businessmen, furthermore, often owe their start to such programs as the Office of Minority Business Enterprises or those of the Great Society.[8]

If we can discount most racial minorities, and—by definition—"Eastern establishment liberals," we still have a long way to go in identifying the New Right, and particularly the "religious New Right." One source for the New Right is suggested by Richard Hofstadter, who describes an American populism that is not necessarily linked to economic privation, but consists of ambitious new entrepreneurs trying to break into established enterprise, politics, and the social world; of a class of cash-conscious farmers and small-town capitalists; and a few heretical individualist businessmen. Alan Crawford adds:

> . . . today's New Right politicians who frequently rail against big business desire only to take away the privileges in the form of subsidies and federal contracts it believes big business receives at the expense of small businessmen and taxpayers generally. Wishing to make every man a capitalist, the New Right sides with the 'new men' of the small business communities and those of the small towns of the heartland rather than the cosmopolitan cities of the Eastern seaboard.[9]

Perhaps this description of populism helps explain the easy slide from pro-family issues into anti-socialism and a "strong America" for those who are depicted as both populist and evangelical or fundamentalist.

People attracted to the New Religious Right are likely to be hometown, latter-day, immigrant Americans who want to achieve middle-class respectability, and to demonstrate their loyalty and patriotism. Perhaps they meet Joseph R. Gusfield's definition of "cultural fundamentalists," who take their values from the traditions of local society, suggests Sen. Thomas J. McIntyre, in his book, *The Fear Brokers*. He observes:

New Rightists sensed that many Americans were beginning to see the lack of spending restraint at all levels of government as evidence of a mass collapse of discipline, order and purpose and as a threat to what they long believed was the right and respectable way to perform as citizens and parents.

The New Right's strategists sensed that a substantial, growing number of people saw 'permissiveness' as the malady weakening the entire moral structure of the nation, from the highest echelons of government down to the individual family structure. It had become plausible to blame permissiveness for a rich roster of evils: corruption in high office; government waste and inefficiency; lack of courage and purpose in foreign policy; a denigration of patriotism; an excess of costly frills and a paucity of standards in public education; welfare cheating and a social atmosphere that encouraged youth rebellion, the generation gap, the counter-culture, the drug culture, sexual promiscuity, disdain for the work ethic, disinterest in religion, and a disinclination to marry and procreate within the sanctions of church and state.[10]

With commendable empathy Senator McIntyre understands these people as basically decent and honest, neither paranoid nor bigoted, but who are anxiety-ridden over what frequently appears to them to be an inexorable assault on their personal value system. He cautions that if they are not to be forfeited to the extremist cause, we must avoid derision and contempt, smugness and condescension, and must acknowledge some elements of truth and fact in their anxiety.

A graphic description of the religious right's sense of alienation and resentment that further illuminates who they are is provided by Martin Marty:

They have felt left out in everyone else's liberation. Women's, black, Chicano, gay, and other liberation movements leave them behind. The textbooks have been changed to accommodate the sensibilities of Jews, homosexuals, women, and the like. The only ethnic stereotypes one can still use and misuse are WASP, redneck, or backwoods and, to a lesser degree, Catholic ethnic. As one such WASP once told me, 'In all their exoduses and liberation plots, I'm Pharoah.' The left-out people not only want in, but they want to run the show. We will make no progress on this issue until the larger public sees the new Christian right as a tribe that feels slighted.[11]

Jeffrey Hadden, therefore, is especially helpful in his description of those who assembled in Dallas:

Perhaps what has angered them most of all is the fact that they don't believe the rest of society, and the government in particular, has taken them seriously. They are tired of being treated as a lunatic fringe or just another interest group that isn't strong enough to be factored into political decisions. Some writers have characterized the New Right Christians as a civil rights group. They mean this not literally, but in a psychological sense. Partly because their own values have held politics to be dirty, and partly because the political process has discounted their importance, they have developed feelings of powerlessness and second-class citizenship.[12]

Similar needs and frustrations were described by Dick Dabney when he observed Pat Robertson's "700 Club" prayer-counseling center, albeit in vastly different language and style:

Greta and the other smiling counselors were into it now, toiling for Jesus, leaning forward into the two-foot-wide tiled cockpits, praying and exhorting, as the desperate called out: the suicidal, drunk, drugged, anxious, and demon-possessed. Their spouses had cheated on them, they were afraid of the Bomb; they were full of cancerous lumps. They had been saved, they had been filled with the Holy Spirit, or they hadn't been, and wanted to be. They were looking for love and a better job and they wanted to step out in faith on those Kingdom Principles and send in the rent money, but were afraid to. And these counselors, with Bibles open, and turning through the thumb-indexed CBN Counseling Manuals that gave answers for every situation, were into it with them—advising, pleading, praying in tongues, hands held up to the oppressively low ceiling—and from time to time checking off the appropriate boxes on the forms—Salvation Forms, Answers-to-Prayers Forms, Holy Baptism Forms, Money Gift Forms—that the systems-analysis experts of Virginia Beach had devised for them, and that would later be fed into the computers, along with the caller's name and address. Above them, from the small television set high on a shelf, Efrem Zimbalist, Jr. was explaining urbanely to Robertson how empty his life had been before he'd found Jesus on Christian TV, and been born again, slain in the Spirit, and given the gift of speaking in tongues.[13]

Alienated, fearful, angry, outraged, frustrated, anxious—they find hope, community, and a reason for being in groups like Christian Voice, Moral Majority, and the "700 Club." Not all of them are lower-middle-class, though figures show a higher percentage of evangelicals are in that category than the general populace, and that a lower percentage have attended college than the public as a whole. Yet, even though the New Right may draw heavily from small town capitalists, Falwell notes that his biggest audiences are in Los Angeles, Philadelphia, Boston and New York, in that order. Dr. George Gerbner, of the Annenberg School of Communications in Philadelphia sees television preachers as having brought these alienated Americans into the mainstream of our society. Jerry Falwell sits in their living room saying just what they, too, have been saying about moral decay in this country, and he invites them to do something about it. He writes back to them, too. And rugged, smiling Pat Robertson chats with successful beauties who love Jesus, with Congressmen who share his sense of the End Times coming but who also seem unafraid, and invites those who are troubled to call him and pledge their dollars for God's bountiful multiplication. Now, not only have they had a Billy Graham and a Jimmy Carter in Washington, but they have a familiar friend on their living room television who assures them that what they think and what they do will make a difference. And it will.

Other "Christian Voices" and Moralities Respond

WELCOME!

We welcome into the political-social-economic arena all who would strive to relate moral and religious convictions to issues in our society. We covet the involvement of evangelicals and all other persons of commitment in the struggle for greater justice and well-being for all persons.

Oklahoma Conference of Churches[1]

This endorsement of the appropriateness of Christians bringing their religious sensitivities into the political process has been uttered forcefully in numerous statements by religious bodies and leaders. The religious right, however, has heard so much criticism, so loudly, that such words of welcome have been drowned out. They need, therefore, to be said again very clearly, as did a group of Christian leaders gathered in Washington from fifteen major American church bodies on October 20, 1980. They registered their agreement with their "companions in the U.S. Christian community" that Christians ought to be engaged in politics and have every right to comment on political issues, to mobilize their church membership to support or oppose legislation, and to provide information on the voting records of office holders.[2]

An editorial voice for the Orthodox Church in America, Fr. John Meyendorff, speaks from a sense of standing in the middle:

It is time, therefore, that both sides transcend the hypocritical self-righteousness with which they accuse their opponents of 'mixing religion with politics.' In fact—and especially in a democratic society—an "apolitical" stance is impossible. Even abstention from voting invites a condonement of the status quo, which is itself a political attitude. On the other hand, the Christian faith, which announces the coming of an eternal Kingdom of God, also implies that the disciples of Jesus are sent into the world in order to transform and transfigure it.[3]

Involvement in politics has been seriously debated within the Presbyterian Church, U.S., for many years, and its Washington office recently reminded its membership of the 1966 General Assembly's words:

> The Christian Church and Christian individuals have one major task in the world: to bear witness to all (persons) in word and act to the judgment, grace and command of God as He is known in the Scriptures of the Old and New Testaments. . . . (This) inevitably and inescapably means that the church and individual Christians will be concerned with the political, social, economic, and cultural life of the world. . . . To abdicate social, political, economic and cultural problems is to say that the Easter message is not true, that God has not and cannot in fact overcome the powers of darkness and evil and other 'lords'.[4]

One of that church's leaders, the President of Union Theological Seminary in New York, Donald W. Shriver, recently stated a related position in *The New York Times*:

> On the one hand, people of faith lose their integrity if they refuse to measure social policy by perspectives rooted in their faith. On the other, a pluralistic society protects its citizens' rights to disagree with each other's faith assumptions, readings of fact and preferred public actions. Freedom of speech includes the freedom to propose a religious argument for a public policy. But no human argument is immune to criticism—from one's neighbor or one's God. . . .
>
> Let us speak publicly about all our reasons for thinking about or doing public business. Who knows? It might help us understand each other, to know where we really disagree and agree, even to teach each other wisdom from our respective inheritances.[5]

In its own wrestle with the issues of citizenship responsibility for Christians, the National Council of Churches of Christ, U.S.A., Executive Committee said,

> Christians have obligations of citizenship to fulfill, particularly the right and duty to vote, as well as the Biblical injunction to work toward a social vision of compassion, justice, and peace. God intends for Christians to pursue the 'things that make for peace and build up the common life', which would include participation in the political process.[6]

In a rather rare tone of unanimity, after having scored the National Council of Churches for hypocrisy in criticizing Falwell, religious columnist Lester Kinsolving agrees:

> The idea that the church should be divorced entirely from civil politics amounts to a suggestion that the church be amoral. For there is no moral issue in existence which has not been the subject of legislation (politics) in either Congress or the various state capitals. By contrast, the idea of keeping the church totally divorced from politics—or totally subservient to the state—has been practiced for years, in the Soviet Union.[7]

One of the few Roman Catholic public statements on issues posed by the religious right makes a similar point:

> There are several points to make about mixing religion and politics. First, we are for it. Politics is the way people's values can influence U.S. social mores. Many of our most cherished American values have a basis in religion, particularly the Judeo-Christian tradition. While the separation of official churches from the state is a great asset to our society, there is no possible way to separate people's religious values from politics. Church-state separation and religion-politics are different things. One is desirable, the other impossible.[8]

Southern Baptist Jimmy Allen, although registering severe criticism of approaches to politics taken by electronic evangelists, speaks a word of hope:

There's an encouraging element in the furor being created by the debate over the place of religious leaders, including electronic evangelists, in the political process. The encouraging fact is that we have reached a stage in our country in which religious experience is being perceived as important. Who would have guessed during the 50's or the 60's that the 80's would find all the presidential candidates giving at least verbal assent to the new birth experience? Close examination will reveal which of them have adequately demonstrated that profession. The fact is, however, that religious experience in an atmosphere of incipient spiritual awakening is a political asset. That's good news for our nation.[9]

From another religious quarter, the *Christian Science Monitor* editorializes its appreciation of Christian fundamentalists for bringing issues of decency to public notice:

Many Americans feel deeply the need for a national moral awakening, for a turning back from what is seen to be a more and more permissive society. The fears are not unfounded. No one of the Judeo-Christian faith can fail to be concerned about the widespread immorality, the rise in out-of-wedlock births, the increased use of hard drugs by the young, the growth of pornography, the indecency portrayed in novels, on television, and even flaunted in the news magazines. America indeed needs to be shaken out of its unthinking tolerance of these trends. To the extent that Christian fundamentalists bring these issues to public notice, their efforts have value. An aroused public is a necessary prelude to constructive reform.[10]

Theologian Richard Neuhaus agrees with the *Monitor*'s concern for America's "unthinking tolerance," and he charges that the great threat today is rampant secularism. In his conversation with other religious leaders in a Reformed Judaism symposium, Neuhaus remarked:

What Jerry Falwell is saying is that we are headed toward a totalitarian end unless we can revive those transcendent, those sacred points of reference by which public policy should be informed and checked. What we are dealing with is a conflict of moralities. You do not have one group trying to impose its morality on a presumably value-free and objective process of decision-making.

Those who claim to be value-free and objective are as morality-laden as Jerry Falwell, although perhaps not as reflective about it. What ultimate values do we believe ought to shape the future of America and, consequently, America's role in world history?

Another appreciative word for the positive contribution of conservative evangelicals to politics is made by political scientist Dr. Robert Zwier and Kentucky graduate student Richard Smith:

> Most important, they have created an awareness of the interrelationships between political issues and biblical beliefs, accurately pointing to the reality that basic moral questions are involved in choices about defense budgets, tax reform, civil rights and education. For too long evangelicals have been concerned solely with personal morality while ignoring the impact of public-policy choices on the moral and spiritual health of our society. For too long evangelicals have maintained a cautious distance from the political arena. It is time for Christians to realize that Jesus Christ is Lord of all—and that includes secular politics as well as church matters.
>
> These groups are also correct in their perception that sin is a ubiquitous force. Their call for national and personal repentance may seem strange to many who think of sin as an individual rather than a collective problem, but the very political, economic and social structures of our country are rife with injustice.[11]

Zwier and Smith also added a commendation to these conservative evangelicals for an honest attempt to remain nonpartisan though their core beliefs would necessarily draw them to the Republicans.

A very sober word concerning the extremes of religious response to the problems of political choice was issued in a pastoral letter from the Bishops of the Episcopal Church, as they called attention to apathy:

> Hardly half the American people entitled to vote do so. For Christians, this withdrawal from political responsibility is faithless and immoral. To fail to vote or to be uninformed in voting is a denial of the biblical faith that Jesus Christ is Lord: the Lord of politics, economics, education, and social systems, as well as of our personal and family lives. . . .

Political withdrawal by Christians creates a vacuum that invites the tyranny of those who would use power for discrimination, oppression, and economic barbarism. That is the immorality of political apathy.[12]

With equal sobriety, Millicent Steer Foster in "A Call to Quaker Participation" states the concern of Friends for political participation:

Friends have never been attracted to political parties, as such. We are skeptical of the lumping together of diverse elements, sometimes with less than moral purposes. We do not want to be used as a front of rectitude by those with selfish motives in their use of power. However, both here and in Great Britain, individual Friends have been able to insure freedom of conscience in holding public office, by their advance statements of conviction, which were acceptable to the electorate.[13]

She reminded the Friends of the long-used acts of interview, letter writing, statement issuing, and deputations—"by these lowly acts . . . we see attrition of evil or obsolescent institutions." She quotes Isaac Sharpless:

A long and discouraging process of quiet work always precedes any prominent change for the better. . . . Does anyone think that, had it not been for the labors of Woolman, the sufferings of Garrison, and the writings of Whittier, Abraham Lincoln would ever have issued the Emancipation Proclamation?[14]

These various Christians have sounded a chord of hope, welcome, appreciation, encouragement, imperative, and a sober sense of a task big enough for all to participate. In the criticism that follows, this should not be forgotten.

Seeing Our Own in Another's Sins

Before leaping to criticize, however, we are admonished by Christ to "take the beam out of our own eye." Jerry Falwell, Pat Robertson, James Robison, and other evangelists have been eager to assist. Gary Jarmin of the Christian Voice lobby, for example, says establishment church leaders are "extraordinarily hypocritical. . . . They creep around the corridors of Congress with their collars on backwards, claiming to represent the Lutheran Church or the United Church of Christ or whatever. . . . I'll wager 99 percent of (the members of) those denominations don't have the faintest idea of the things they stand for."[1]

Rather than devote more space to further accusations against "secular humanist liberals," it is more spiritually significant to hear the second thoughts the phenomenon of the religious right is inducing in other parts of the broad Christian community. Groups like Moral Majority and Christian Voice perform a function similar to a Hirschberg cartoon. Their political behavior is an exaggeration of what other Christian groups believe is appropriate. One recognizes in their distortions some aspects of oneself, not all of which are admirable, and one sees those aspects more clearly because of the caricature's exaggerations. Some of the behavior most disturbing to mainline Christians, therefore, is likely to be caricatures of their own offenses.

This has begun to be sensibly and sensitively recognized within the National Council of Churches, for just one example. As its national staff and officers began to engage in discussions about the religious right, they had to undergo considerable self-analysis. The Council was slow to enter public debate and criticism on the subject, because it recognized that the differences in approach were subtle, and that in certain respects its own organization was not as distinctively different in practice as it professed to be. Task teams for preparing position statements and for thinking through long-term responses to the challenges from the right have revealed the following assorted self-criticisms with no attempt to reflect a consensus:

> Finding arrogance in others, the National Council of Churches becomes sensitive to its own spiritual arrogance. Seeing Moral Majority captive to a right wing ideology, it acknowledges its own fascination with liberal and left-leaning answers and strategies for the world's ills. Rejecting the simplicity of social analysis of the religious right, the Council is determined to be more stringent in its own

analysis. The scriptural selectivity of electronic church evangelists reminds other Christians of their own selectivities. While noting the national provincialism of the religious right, the Council rejoices in the scope of its own internationalism but recognizes omissions in its domestic concerns. The Council has sought to be open to the needs of women, of minorities, and of people undergoing socio-economic repression, and the opening of those doors has unwittingly slammed shut other doors. While advocating religious liberty, establishment liberals have ignored the very religious groups who now most clamor to be heard. Although not nearly so engrossed in social causes to the exclusion of other ministries as those who do not know the immense scope of its full program often charge, the National Council of Churches is aware that, partly through the vagaries of its own structure, it has worked diligently in some areas but not in other equally valid areas.

Such self-criticism and spiritual self-searching are no small gain. They do not represent a "failure of nerve" or a withdrawal from deeply-rooted social justice concerns. A reassessment of the meaning and theological sources for ecumenism had already been well underway in the National Council of Churches. Rather, it is the thoughtful examination of the mode and scope of Council work that is being prodded by the public response to the religious right. A sampling of the nudge to self-inquiry described above is evident in the following quotes:

—As your bishops, we speak out now because the silence of the conventional churches is partly to blame for the impact of this new coalition of strident voices. . . .[2] (Episcopal Bishops)

—This is a time to listen. To see whether we have contributed unthinkingly to a way of life that makes the fundamentalist rightism plausible to so many. Have we indulged only in our doubts, been simple relativists, unready to hear others?[3] (Martin Marty, Lutheran)

—(On militarism and defense of the Constitution by Presidents) Are there ways that we can be more practically helpful to our Presidents in dealing with this particular realm of Caesar?[4] (Wilma Kern, Quaker)

—We must admit that we do not always clearly understand God's Word, and that we do not fathom the complexities of these policy issues. Every group of Christians, not only the conservative ones . . . must refrain from the arrogance of presumed omniscience and must adopt an attitude of humility befitting our sinful nature.[5] (Zweier and Smith, Evangelicals)

—In our efforts to coalesce into a majority, I think we must confess we have at times been too one-sided and lost sight of essence. The emotional experience must be tied in with the ethical in society.[6] (Bishop Frank Madison Reid, Africian Methodist Episcopalian)

—Evangelicals will subject the gospel of Jesus to unnecessary rejection by others if they identify it with any political program. Liberals and radicals have sometimes made the same mistake.[7] (D.W. Shriver, Union Theological Seminary)

—(Liberals) are the ones who have driven us into this current dilemma by trying to purge American life of religion and values—by creating a 'naked public square' where anything goes.[8] (Richard Neuhaus, *Worldview*)

—It may be that this country needs a right-wing scare badly. How else to wake up the clergyman, the deacons, the decent churchgoers who were such a force for racial and social justice in the early 1960's?[9] (Carl T. Rowan, journalist)

—In fighting the horrors of racism, discrimination and oppression, the liberals of the sixties were (and still are) often unaware of the danger of jumping on the bandwagon of secular revolutionary ideologies whose ultimate goal is not to protect human dignity, but to destroy it. . . . The real danger for Christians lies not in political activity as such, but in a loss of their Christian identity.[10] (Fr. Meyendorff, Orthodox)

—Many critics of the Moral Majority and Christian Voice single-issue politics were, in fact, pioneers of it and are crying alarm about violations of principles of separation of church and state when they themselves have been roundly criticized in the past.[11] (Sen. Mark Hatfield)

—. . . many liberation theologies are as fanatic and unresponsive to criticism, as theologically sure of themselves as is the force we are talking about today.[12] (Martin Marty)

—We liberals are often too sanctimonious, entirely too aggrandizing in our self-perception. We think that we hold a patent on decency. We do not.[13] (Rabbi A.M. Schindler)

—I know that we lost, not because we ran away, but because on a number of key issues they were right and we didn't have the imagination or the nerve to come up with convincing alternatives.[14] (Richard Neuhaus)

Mainline churches are already troubled by declining membership, which has been identified through research as a problem caused chiefly by not holding onto their young (a trend that shows some slight amelioration recently). The prevailing individualistic social values of young people seem to loosen not only their ties with family, but also those with institutions and community life generally. While not ready to buy the rigid, government-enforced answers of the Christian right, mainline church leaders are no less concerned about "the family," including the whole human family-community. Clearly, the "pro-family movement" cannot pre-empt all concern for families. It is ironic that women's issues have been under the heaviest attack from the religious new right, even though women comprise a disproportionate majority of evangelicals. Have the churches failed to demonstrate their long-standing concern for family, and their concern for women who suffer from the wreckage that zealots at either end of the spectrum of women's issues have wrought? This and other questions posed by self-criticism are religious challenges for the broad Christian community.

Religious Challenges to the Religious Right

With questions and concerns still healthily fermenting their own efforts to live under the judgment and grace of the Gospel, the various religious groups that do not identify with the religious right have begun to challenge it with Gospel imperatives. Although several groupings are certainly possible, the following selection of critical issues highlights the most frequent and impassioned charges:

> An inadequate agenda based upon Scriptural selectivity.
> Promulgation of an elitist patriotism which encourages militarism and provincialism.
> A failure to respect diversity in American society, basic to religious liberty.
> Threatening democratic process through passionate, vindictive certitude.
> Endangering the credibility and mission of the church.

Inadequate Agenda

Dr. Donald Dayton of the Northern Baptist Theological Seminary forcefully addressed an evangelical concern for the inadequacy of the Moral Majority agenda based upon an inadequate reading of Scripture:

> I do question . . . the claim of Moral Majority to represent 'biblical morality'. Concern about homosexuality, for example, permeates this group's literature; yet the Bible speaks directly to this issue in only a handful of texts, several of which are obscure and difficult. But there are literally hundreds of biblical texts that speak of justice and of God's concern for the poor. Faith that does not grasp the pervasiveness of this theme in Scripture is not biblical faith.[1]

This echoes black evangelical activist Tom Skinner, who says, "There are more than 300 verses in the Bible on the commitment to the poor, to justice and righteousness, but they are silent on that."[2] District of Columbia's Rev. Walter Fauntroy objects to "the application by the so-called 'Moral Majority' of religious principles to a very narrow range of secondary policy issues, while blatantly opposing the application of religious principles to a broad range of primary political issues." Fauntroy speaks of "our Lord's inaugural address":

> The Spirit of the Lord God is upon me; because he hath anointed me to preach good news to the poor, he hath sent me to heal the

brokenhearted, to preach deliverance to the captives, and recovery of sight to the blind, to set at liberty them that are bruised.

He feels that "ultra-right wing forces" are taking advantage of "many well-meaning born-again Christians" by using Christianity "against the very concerns for the poor that are at the heart of our Judeo-Christian faith."[3] Another black religious leader, Bishop Frank Madison Reid, comments:

> Many of those who populate this religious position want prayer in schools but don't seem to mind too much if low tax rates wreck the school system. Yes, they want prayer in schools even if the schools are inadequate and segregated.[4]

The ecumenical statements in the Appendix all sound this theme. The "Call to Responsible Christian Action" statement by Evangelicals for Social Action also says in part:

> Today we are increasingly concerned that the resurgence of evangelical concern for public policy is not sufficiently biblical. There is a danger that evangelicals will be preoccupied with a selective list of concerns that does not reflect truly biblical priorities and emphases. . . .
>
> We call on all Christians concerned for our society to search out biblical principles to govern and direct that concern, and to allow their inherited prejudices to be judged and transformed by these principles. Among these we would especially call attention to the following:
>
> 1. Each individual is created in the image of God and is the object of his loving concern. Anything which degrades or does violence to the integrity of the human personality is antithetical to divine purposes.
> 2. God commands us to be especially concerned for the weak and powerless in society. . . .
> 3. God has appointed us to be stewards of his creation, even though it is presently marred by sin. We are to care for our physical environment in as loving and responsible a fashion as possible because it belongs to Him. Biblical teaching on justice summons us to work against the individualistic, materialistic idolatry of our age, which has led both to despoliation and depletion of God's

creation and to an unjust distribution of wealth, power, and income within our country and among the nations of the world.
4. Our Lord calls His followers to be peacemakers. . . . We must endeavor in every way possible to promote peace among individual human beings, social classes, and even nations.[5]

Sen. Mark Hatfield joins other evangelicals in this criticism, as he says in the *Congressional Record*:

Many evangelicals share my concern that the grievous sins of our society are militarism and materialism, rather than the Taiwan Treaty, the Equal Rights Amendment or the Panama Canal.[6]

An executive with the National Council of Churches, Dr. William F. Fore, sees a bias toward the affluent in Falwell's selection of issues:

As H. Richard Niebuhr said, all knowledge is conditioned by the standpoint of the knower. That is, where you stand depends on where you sit. And Jerry Falwell's audience is sitting on top of the most healthy, luxury-laden and prodigiously wasteful society the world has ever known.

Thus his opposition to federal funding of abortion limits the options of the pregnant unwed black teen-ager in Harlem but not of the pregnant unwed middle-class white teen-ager in Indianapolis. His call for greater military spending provides increased income for millions of American armament workers and decreased economic aid for the poor of this nation and the Third World.[7]

A Roman Catholic voice joins the chorus of concern over Christians being coopted to the issues of right-wing politicians:

For example, it's difficult to see how people who are pro-life, against killing the unborn, could also advocate the death penalty, more nuclear weapons and a belligerent military/foreign policy that is likely to get us into the horrible killings of warfare. And it is difficult, for example, to see how the Christian gospel, which professes works of mercy, compassion and help for the poor, squares with regressive taxes and slashed welfare budgets that punish the poor. Yet the right-wing religious/political leaders are connecting these contradictory positions.[8]

From the President of the Union of American Hebrew Congregations comes a related charge:

> Their ideological banner is wide. They seek to Christianize America, to make this a republic ruled by Christ. Yet they give their religion a narrow definition. They are pro-family and pro-life. But they ignore and even oppose such religious principles as stewardship of our resources, and care for the poor, and justice and peace; as a case in point, they are violently opposed to the U.S. ratification of the Genocide convention. High on their priorities also are some issues which are more political than moral and come straight from the right-wing lexicon: Government spending, the abrogation of the Taiwan security treaty, Panama Canal and the devaluation of the dollar.[9]

Christians within the denominations that compose the National Council of Churches are sometimes drawn into the religious right, raising challenges to their own denominational programs and priorities. A recent challenge to the program and practices of the United Methodist Church was led by Mr. David Jessup with the encouragement and publication assistance of the Good News conservative group within the United Methodist Church. Responding to the charges, the United Methodist Communications wrote:

> . . . We are not simply discussing some apolitical need for theological and political 'balance' in our denomination. We are nearing the center of a debate between different worldviews. As change swirls around us, some persons cling to an understanding of history and the role of our nation that seems to be fading. Such persons are deeply troubled by the shifting of power they see in the world and are fearful. Contrast this to a worldview which stresses government's and people's efforts toward the alleviation of injustice and suffering, the recognition of new nations, the ending of all forms of colonialism, the rights of all races and both sexes to equality and, thus, full humanity—and the rights of the environment as well.[10]

Indeed, to read the materials from ecumenical groups and from Christian Voice, is to experience two different worlds, almost two different Bibles.

The choice of issues also influences the way "moral criteria" are determined for political candidates. This can be seen in the list of Congressional votes that constitute the "morality rating" of candidates by Christian Voice. On theological and ethical grounds an ecumenical group of church leaders objected to these moral criteria as a rating instrument, saying:

> We believe the narrow range of issues selected by such groups as the Christian Voice and the Christian Voters' Victory Fund for the purpose of rating members of Congress represents ideological preferences rather than the breadth of responsible Christian positions.[9]

This concern for the narrow gate through which a candidate walks in order to be judged moral is expressed by the *Christian Science Monitor*:

> The results can be incongruous, and often hardly moral in themselves. Such an able senator as John Glenn, for instance, who is an elder in the Presbyterian church, is rated zero by one ultra-conservative organization. Congressman Richard Kelly, implicated in the Abscam bribery investigation, merits 100. . . .
>
> A moral America encompasses more than an obligation to protect human life—and abortion is a practice we oppose but which involves such complex issues as to be best left to individual conscience and choice. Morality involves the whole tone of society—the integrity of government leaders, the ethics of corporate business, and the sensitivity of schools, universities, news media, and the arts and entertainment industry to purifying the nation's cultural as well as physical environment. It means addressing such problems as justice for blacks and other minorities, equal rights for women (recognized even by many opponents of ERA), and training of the unemployed. Is it morally tolerable that millions of people cannot find work, that joblessness among black youth, in particular, runs a high 40 percent?[12]

To illustrate the importance of which issues are chosen as the moral criteria, Zwier and Smith contrasted senatorial ratings by Christian

Voters Victory Fund with those by Bread for the World. For CVVF, Sens. Cranston and Culver received 0 ratings, while Sens. Helms and Humphrey got 100; in Bread for the World, Cranston and Culver received 100 ratings, while Helms and Humphrey both were marked 0!

Is sin that difficult to define in Scripture? John Danforth, a Republican senator from Missouri and an ordained Episcopal minister, reminds us that "Norms do exist for determining the applicability of religious principles to political commentary, and for Jews and Christians those norms are scriptural. The job of the religious commentator on the political scene is to reflect on contemporary events in the light of scriptural tradition." He finds little help in the Bible for deciding whether there should be a Department of Education, but "what is found in Scripture, over and over again, is a boundless concern that justice be done to the needy—the poor, the fatherless, the widows."[13]

Evangelical scholar Robert E. Webber, in his soon to be published manuscript *The Moral Majority: Right or Wrong?*, finds Falwell's uncritical support for the free enterprise system too optimistic a reading of human nature. He claims that all human systems are tainted by human selfishness and greed and the "powers" of evil, based upon a biblical view of humanity. In Falwell's *Listen America* "morality, economics, and politics are so intertwined in American government that it is impossible to talk of one without the other," says Webber. Although Falwell gives no biblical argument for the free enterprise system, he reads the Bible through the contemporary conservative economics bends of Milton Friedman, Jesse Helms, and William E. Simon. Webber's manuscript, to be printed by Cornerstone Books, Westchester, Illinois, 1981, makes a case for the evangelical centrist, who avoids the extremes of both Moral Majority and the World Council of Churches while pursuing the goals of social transformation dear to both political agendas.

Not only the selection of issues but the way those issues are stated is the concern of some Christians. When one responds to a questionnaire asking, "Do you believe that abortion on demand should be legal?" one might well be against the very permissive "abortion on demand" but not opposed to abortion in all cases.

How will one's "yes" or "no" be interpreted? Or, if asked, "Do you favor more or less Federal government?" how does a conservative Christian reply who wants the government to deny homosexuals the right to teach in public schools, who wants "right to life" and prayer in public school constitutional amendments, and who wants government controls on pornography? When asked, "Will you support pro-family legislation?" how does one express one's deep concern about the problems of American families without becoming identified with one ideological perspective on what constitutes "pro-family"? These questionnaire questions are samples suggested in a manual "A Program for Political Participation of Church-Going Christians" distributed at the January, 1981 evangelical convocation in Washington, D.C. by the religious right.

Unsound biblical scholarship is the concern of Bishop Anthony Bosco, chancellor of the Catholic Diocese of Pittsburgh. One reason for his concern is the emphasis upon "pre-tribulation rapture," a doctrine with very shaky scholarship that is accepted chiefly by fundamentalists and is a mainstay of electronic evangelists. In a nuclear age this is an appealing doctrine, because it not only provides a comforting interpretation of possible nuclear holocaust, but it also delivers ("raptures") those who believe into heaven before the blast. One can therefore hope that the end is coming soon, even provoke it, without fear of personal, bodily harm. The need for such a belief supersedes the necessity of learning whether or not it stands up to careful scriptural interpretation.[14]

In summarizing this challenge to the religious right, it is necessary to distinguish between the efficiency and effectiveness of their single-issue political networks, and their claim to encompass a "moral agenda for the eighties." Single-issue groups that work to enact a particular piece of legislation have legitimacy and many groups of various ideological persuasions have used this approach in the past. Not every religious group involved in politics must necessarily tackle *all* the issues that Christians should care about. Indeed mainline churches have probably erred on the side of trying to address too many issues. Selections of priorities has always involved cruel choices with limited resources. But when one is claiming to define who are the moral candidates worthy of Christians' support, the definition of "moral" must encompass the major biblical themes that constitute "doing justice, loving mercy, and walking humbly with God," or the morality being espoused is itself morally deficient.

Elitist Patriotism

Most Americans love their country, even those who spend an inordinate amount of time criticizing it. Liberals may well have overdone criticism in their zeal for making their country better, assuming that the unspoken word of affection is taken for granted. Jerry Falwell does not make that mistake. He denounces certain sins of America with more vitriolic vigor than any except the most radical youth of the sixties. But he does it with flags waving, pledges of allegiance, and "I love America" rallies. His zeal prompted the Episcopal bishops to write to their flock:

> As Christians we share some important commitments with the so-called Moral Majority: to the home, to the family, to the Bible—though our understanding of reverence for Scripture compels us to resist any narrow or bullying use of biblical texts. But with our brothers and sisters of the popular TV ministry we too cherish God and country. The stars and stripes of our national banner are conspicuous in many Episcopal Churches, and we offer Eucharist on the 4th of July.[15]

Episcopal Bishop Paul Moore also described loyalty to the Declaration of Independence, the Bill of Rights, the Constitution, and the flag when he addressed the church on "True Conservatism."

> These symbols, these words, these frail bits of cloth conserve our faith in the principles upon which our nation was founded: Individual worth, freedom, political and economic justice and peace. True conservatism is the preservation of such principles and such structures as allow the life of our nation and our Church to flow free and unhindered to the glory of God and love for all His people, for the building of His kingdom, and for the bringing of peace to all the world.[16]

On the other hand, Zwier and Smith judge Falwell's singing of the national anthem to be a bit off-key, because they find the claim that the U.S. is *the* instrument to accomplish the will of God suspect:

> There is no doubt that God could use, and probably is using, this nation for His purposes, but the claim of these groups carries with it a historical and cultural relativism that seeks to interpret God's plan within a framework of flag-waving nationalism. Their claim further excludes God's use of other countries with strong Judeo-Christian foundations or other religious tenets and ignores the possibility that even 'godless' nations are instruments which God can use.[17]

In another setting I also took issue with a divinely-blessed nationalism:

> Presbyterians, who believe in the sovereignty of God, affirm that our nation already *is* 'under God,' whether or not it behaves or declares itself to be under God's authority. Furthermore, we believe that *all* nations are 'under God,' as human institutions expressing our creaturehood, loved, blessed, and judged by our Creator.
>
> One of our obligations as Christians is to view our citizenship in a nation of our own making as part of a world and universe of God's making. We must ask not only what is good for our country, but how our country can be good for God's world. 'For God so loved the *world* that He gave His only begotten Son. . . .' We are enjoined in love to ask of our leaders and our laws, 'Who is helped? Who is injured? Who is left out? Who is heard? Who is ignored?' When we vote, we do not vote to serve only ourselves or only our country, if we see our citizenship as an act of Christian discipleship.[18]

If the attempt to describe those who are drawn into the religious right has any accuracy, one should not be surprised to find an international outlook missing from their viewpoint. Few would-be international travellers or have much experience with those who are, so it is from the vantage point of unusual privilege that some Christians are able to hear how the God bless America patriotism sounds to Christians in other countries.

The dangers of being an "elect nation" or an "elect people" ought still to be very much alive for Americans who remember Germany's aspirations under Hitler. Although some people are quick to see parallels with fascism, Martin Marty is cautious about making premature judgments:

> All things being equal, our political pluralism is rich enough and our human resources resourceful and resilient enough that we can keep from being overwhelmed now, as we have kept from such outcomes before. Now not all things are always equal, and the circumstances of life could vastly change. The world is not moving toward toleration but away from it. The age is not, in many ways, a time of ecumenical convergence but of tribal divergence and separation (and the new American Christian right did not invent that) . . . Should there be barn-burning, back-busting depression in America in a decade; should there be an outburst of violence and terrorism which citizens would wish to put down by creating a surveillance society; should there be a total social(ist) reorganization of the economy—how would we legitimize the shifts? It never seems likely to me that we would do it through Marx or Mao. We would use Jesus and call the program Christian Democracy.[19]

It is also an easy step from "elect" nationalism to strident militarism, as Moral Majority demonstrates. They justify their desire for superior American power in the world, as opposed to a balance of power, by insisting that the United States (as an "elect nation") has special claims to morality and God's guidance. The Tulsa Metropolitan Ministry statement charges that,

> Moral Majority has aligned itself with those who define national security in terms of military supremacy and nuclear first-strike capability and with those who define national interest in terms of dominance. First, we question whether or not any nation has the right to claim morality for itself. Second, along with several religious bodies, we question whether or not national security is enhanced by escalation of the arms race. Third, we see that increased military spending can only mean that more people go hungry.

Robert McAfee Brown has done a careful analysis of Falwell's book *Listen, America!* in which Brown documents a massive inconsistency between faith in God's ability to save us from "godless Communism" and the need for military superiority. Quoting Falwell on p. 106 of *Listen, America!* (italics added):

If God is on our side, no matter how militarily superior the Soviet Union is, they could never touch us. God would miraculously protect America.

Brown comments shrewdly:

> Thus, Falwell makes the choice clear: It's either God—or weapons. And then he chooses . . . weapons! Weapons on almost every page, God on page 106. Who(m) does he really trust? The only consistent thesis seems to be, 'Yes, we can trust God to save us miraculously, if we turn back to Him, but just to be on the safe side, let's arm ourselves to the teeth.' Whatever that is, it isn't trust in God.[20]

Another caution, voiced by Mark Hatfield, is the idealization of American history by the religious right:

> Many Christian conservatives have, I think, unwittingly exaggerated the role of religion in American history, making America God's nation of the New Covenant. An organization called Citizens for God and Country, and preachers influenced by it, claim (our country) exclusively for Christian religion and purport that all others are 'against the law.' It is good to remind ourselves that many of our founding fathers were Deists, children of the Enlightenment, not the Reformation.[21]

Martin Marty picks up Hatfield's last comment with this elucidation:

> They laud the founders of the nation, the signers of the Declaration of Independence, not more than one or two of whom could have been members of any of their churches. One or two of the signers were Presbyterian in the rather conventional mold; almost all the rest were a sort of Episcopalian or Congregationalist whom the fundamentalists today would call humanists, Unitarians or even secular humanists. . . . In effect, the fundamentalist political movement is trying to make second-class citizens of everyone who isn't that, and that the founders deliberately set out not to do it.[22]

Although much should be said about the colonial period (and the expectations of some early settlers that they were founding the New Israel), there is not enough space here to do so. In light of this the reader would be well served by turning to Robert Bellah's *The*

Broken Covenant. Other aspects of the idealization of history can be picked up in an exchange of reader's letters in *The New York Times,* in which Richard Armstrong replies to Gary Potter:

> Mr. Potter . . . says that our laws, policies and public ceremonies used to reflect the values, beliefs and principles of Christianity—and they should again. This is nostalgia for a Golden Age that never existed.
>
> What about slavery, the corruption that followed the Civil War, our Mexican War, Indian wars, the Spanish-American War, Vietnam? Did these reflect the views of Christians—or was it only the despised 'secularists' who perpetrated these imperialistic policies? Was it the secular humanists who made it hard for Mr. Potter's ancestors and my own when they arrived in this country, only to be put down by the Know-Nothings? Is the anti-Semitism in our society merely the work of those who reject religion?[23]

From the Church of the Brethren comes another history lesson. Concerned over continued references to a return to something that never was, a *Messenger* article says:

> History does not support the belief that America has ever been Christian—or that the founders intended it to be. Most of them were concerned about freedom—including *religious freedom*—and would never have agreed to use government to force a religion, creed or doctrine on anyone.
>
> As one critic of 'Washington, for Jesus' expressed it: 'I reject the idea that America needs *to go back* to God. The America I know never was *with* God. Unless God approved of George Washington owning slaves, Thomas Jefferson throwing one of his mulatto children into the Potomac, Puritans burning heretics at the stake and 'Jim Crow' ruling the the South.' Indeed, America has always needed to hear the gospel. It still does. But the government can never become a vehicle by which that gospel is proclaimed.

The author then reminds readers of the Church of the Brethren 1967 statement entitled "The Church, the State and Christian Citizenship," which says in part:

> As citizens, we are called to oppose any encroachment by the church upon the rightful functioning of the state. As Christians whose

highest commitment is to God, we are called to oppose any encroachment by the state upon the divinely instituted mission of the church and its members. Christians, acting individually and corporately in the affairs of the State, must be found "speaking boldly for the Lord, who bore witness to the word of his grace, granting signs and wonders to be done. . . . (Acts 14:3)"[24]

Issues, therefore, of religious liberty and respect for diversity in our pluralistic society become the third area of concern.

Lack of Respect for Diversity

Senator Mark Hatfield submitted a guest editorial to the *Oregon Statesman Journal* which so impressed Senator Javits that he requested it to be printed in the *Congressional Record*.[25] A Jewish senator was honoring the thinking of an evangelical Christian on the prickly question of religion and politics. Hatfield had described the lack of moral and philosophical cohesion in our social order that could result in atomization, simplistic mass movements, or apathy. He argued there was a need for an effective, legitimizing national framework that would avert polarization, but he counseled against the use of religion as a mere "glue." Calling for a spiritual renewal that was genuinely religious, Hatfield hoped that the pluralism of this country could continue to be respected, without succumbing to what Meg Greenfield called the "lowest common denominator generalities" where "any indecency, outrage or pathological assault on our sense of rightness" is seen only as a civil liberties problem.

Simply dubbing one's position as the moral majority opinion of the country does not adequately address Hatfield's sensitive concern for some "holding center" in our society. The Tulsa Metropolitan Ministry statement said:

We feel that all persons of faith must discern what is moral. No one group can claim that its historically relative position on morality is God's own definition of morality. Second, we know of no religious tradition which systematically equates morality with the viewpoint of a majority.

Bishop Maximos of the Greek Orthodox Diocese commented: "The famous Moral Majority is actually a minority, consisting mostly of fundamentalists. It cannot speak for all of us. I disagree with many points on their stand." While agreeing with Hatfield that America must have a strong moral and spiritual foundation, the *Christian Science Monitor* opposed the limited definition of morality, and the imposition of that morality upon society by the religious right, as a "theocratic force."

> But morality must be built within the thoughts and lives of individuals and then translated into the nation's laws and policies through the democratic process. It cannot be imposed by the state either on individuals or on nations. And it is not Christian morality that lapses into bigotry, self-righteousness, or pious preachiness.[26]

"There is a lot about the movement's inflexibility, intolerance and passion for annihilation that makes me think of the Great Inquisition and the Dark Ages," said Bishop Reid of Columbia, South Carolina. And former Senator Harold Hughes of Iowa, who has left politics to be an evangelistic lay minister, spoke up for those who espouse no religion:

> I don't like the suggestion that the United States is a Christian country. The right not to believe must be upheld or the right to believe will be threatened.[27]

The Washington Interreligious Staff Council also addressed the issue of the political functioning of religious groups within a pluralistic society in its statement that criticized the Washington for Jesus rally.[28]

Because many issues of morality have to do with "pro-family" concerns, the very concept of "family" is a subject of debate within a pluralistic society, as was certainly dramatized at the recent White House Conference on the Family. The Tulsa Metropolitan Ministry statement charged:

> We believe that the Moral Majority's stereotype of the family ignores the large number of those who are not in a traditional family lifestyle and does not adequately take into account the social forces affecting

the family. It also seems to us that the family is used by the Moral Majority to deemphasize or avoid the Scriptural mandates to seek justice and to meet the needs of those who are different from ourselves.[29]

Bishop Reid expressed a similar concern when he said, "Many one parent families are more intact than many two parent families. Cohesiveness of the family is determined by the quality and intensity of the relationships among family members and not whether there is a father in the home." And Episcopalian Bishop Paul Moore claimed:

> These forces of the right use the slogan 'pro-family' as a weapon against women's rights and gay rights. 'Pro-family' to them means lack of compassion for broken families and all other hapless people who do not have the blessing, usually through no fault of their own, of a tight and happy nuclear family.[30]

Census figures show a sizeable portion of the population to be one-person households (22%) and two-person households (30.7%). Female heads of families have increased from 8.7% for white women in 1960 to 11.5% in 1978, and from 22.4% for black and other minority women in 1960 to 36% in 1978. The divorce rate in 1960 was 2.2 per 1,000 population, and it more than doubled to 5.1 in 1978. These statistics document great changes in the general public's expectations about family life. They also include much pain, failure, loneliness, agony and irresponsibility in broken and disrupted human relationships. Is the only word from the church to the people who suffer the painful aspects of these statistics one of judgment? What about the gospel of love and forgiveness, of salvation and healing? And what about the economic and social forces that need to be taken into account?

An even greater test of pluralism in our society is the attitude toward persons of other faiths. Rabbi Marc H. Tanenbaum, in a paper written at the time Jimmy Carter was running as a "born again" Christian, assured his readers that there are indeed authentic differences and conflicting claims between religious communities. He urged that those relating to public policy should be openly confronted and discussed. Remembering that Roger Williams left the "enforced establishment of evangelical orthodoxy in the Massachusetts Bay colony" in 1638 to form a new colony in Rhode Island that honored the Baptist tradition of religious liberty and freedom of conscience, he recounted Williams' celebrated parable of the ship:

> There goes many a ship to sea, with many hundred souls in one ship, whose weal and woe is common; and is a true picture of common-wealth, or any human combination or society. It hath fallen out some times that both Papists and Protestants, Jews and Turks may be embarked into one ship. Upon which supposal, I affirm that all the liberty of conscience that ever I pleaded for, turns upon these two hinges, that none of the Papists, Protestants, Jews or Turks be forced to come to the ship's prayer or worship nor compelled from their own particular prayers or worship if they practice any.[31]

Roger Williams would mount an impassioned speech today on the issue of prayer in the public schools.

Applying Roger Williams' respect for religious liberty to the present situation, Rabbi Tanenbaum remarked in a Reformed Judaism sponsored symposium:

> I am concerned about the tendency of many people in local communities to vote for born-again Christians only. Falwell rejected that finally, but it was like taking the genie out of the bottle; once it got into the mainstream he had no control over what began happening in local communities. You had campaigns all over America to seize the local political machinery, to vote into office born-again Christians only because that was supposed to assure that there was going to be a return to some basic morality.
>
> Unfortunately, Jerry Falwell does not know the history of his own church, does not know the history of the Baptists in the United States and the incredible persecution, even murder, they suffered in upholding religious pluralism and freedom of conscience. He seems to perceive the whole of human experience essentially as a conflict between the forces of Christ and Antichrist. That rhetoric was used in some of the political campaigns. . . . When the Rev. James Robison spoke in Dallas of the sin of secular humanism, "that the secular humanists stand at the shoulder of Satan," that they are in league with the Antichrist, and that the obligation is not just to defeat them but to demolish them, you can see the basis of religious war.

Tanenbaum is concerned about judging political performance on the basis of certain Biblically-derived standards (like the "morality ratings") and fears that Article Six of the Constitution, which says there must not be any religious test for holding office, may be violated. This concern is not new. It was foremost in a joint news conference called in October, 1976, by four religious leaders from Roman Catholic, evangelical, Protestant Episcopal, and Jewish traditions to protest both a religious test for candidates and the movement toward electing "real Christians only." The statement said:

> [Americans] cannot share the underlying assumptions: that candidates for office are to be judged on grounds other than their political and civic qualifications—and that non-Christian believers, nonbelievers, or even Christians with a different religious commitment are less qualified, trustworthy or patriotic.[32]

The statement warned:

> Freedom of religions has also made possible our pluralistic society, with its capacity for negotiating and reconciling religious conflicts and differences that have so often plunged other societies into strife, misery and bloodshed.
>
> To create religious voting blocs on the American scene would be to discard these historic achievements—to invite a return of religious strife or oppression. It could bring us back to the conditions of Colonial times, when theocratic rulers withheld religious liberty from the people.[33]

Background material for this 1976 statement described the activities of the Christian Freedom Foundation, Third Century Publishers, Christian Embassy, Campus Crusade for Christ, and Intercessors for America, all of which were seen to have "interlocking directorates." A current bit of background evidence for concern over candidate qualifications is found in Vernon McLellen's "Believer's Checklist for Choosing a Candidate," in the November, 1980 issue of *Christian Life*. It lists 26 qualification questions for selecting a candidate, beginning with "Does he/she trust in the Lord?" and "Does he honor the Bible and seek God's wisdom?"

and, thirdly, "Does he put God first?" It then lists a series of ethical questions, and only at number nineteen does it ask, "Does he evaluate the facts fairly? Is he experienced, knowledgeable and qualified to hold office?"

The issue of anti-Semitism, however, is more delicate than the call for religious liberty. A background paper on the New Right prepared for the American Jewish Committee has found that

> . . . no known anti-Semites are identified with the New Right, and the principal groups have made no public overtures to the several Klan and Nazi groups who endorse New Right positions on various issues. While the history of American populism is replete with attempts by populist leaders to scapegoat Jews, this latter day populist movement has no discernible anti-Semitic component. Its hate objects are the 'Eastern Elitist Establishment,' and the Rockefellers.[34]

Distinguishing between the New Right and the religious New Right, the paper continues:

> In contrast, the religious New Right, indifferent to or unfamiliar with Jewish concerns or sensibilities, is pro-Israel. Fundamentalist theology holds that there will be an ingathering of Jews to biblical Palestine and that the establishment of a Jewish commonwealth is a condition precedent to the second coming of Jesus. The state of Israel has received support on the air, from the pulpit and in the newspapers from fundamentalist ministers. Many have visited Israel and met with Prime Minister Begin and other Israeli leaders. As a group with an estimated 50 million followers, the religious New Right potentially is a strong American ally of the Jewish State.[35]

It is such doctrines as the pre-tribulation rapture—and post-tribulation rapture—that Rabbi Tanenbaum gently and cogently reprimands in his 1976 statement:

> Jews naturally resent any approach which reduces them—or the State of Israel—to theological abstractions, preliminary stages in someone else's drama of redemption.[36]

Reform Jewish leader Rabbi Schindler forcefully agrees:

> After all, the deepest reasons for the support given to Israel by the evangelical fundamentalists are theologically self-serving. As *they* read Scripture, Jesus cannot return for the Second Coming until all the Jews are regrouped in the whole of their Biblical land and then are converted to Christianity. Only true believers can enter the gate of heaven. Devout Jews, if they refuse to accept Jesus, will not be permitted beyond those pearly gates. They will be buried beneath Mount Zion once the Newer Israel replaces the old. . . . This is their apocalyptic vision in all its fullness: they seek our extinction as a particular people. Why then in heaven's name should we give them recognition?[37]

The background paper of the American Jewish Committee reminds its readers:

> Jews are wary, recognizing that a strong anti-Jewish strain has permeated the fundamentalist clergy over the years. Out of their ranks came such notorious anti-Semites as the Rev. Gerald K. Smith and the Rev. Gerald Winrod, the 'jayhawk' Nazi.[38]

And, it adds, Dr. Bailey Smith did nothing to assuage their fears.

There is some dispute about the danger of anti-Semitism among various Jewish leaders. On one side, Rabbi Schindler of the Union of American Hebrew Congregations told his board of trustees that right-wing Christian fundamentalism was fostering anti-Semitism by creating a divisive climate of opinion hostile to religious tolerance. In response, the board resolved that the insistence on only one brand of politics being acceptable to God was "a clear and present danger to the traditions of American pluralism and a threat to the fabric of American life, to a democratic society, to Jewish values and to the security of American Jewry." Siding with Schindler, Ira Glasser of the American Civil Liberties Union finds the "so-called 'Christian' agenda of groups like the Moral Majority" in fact an "anti-civil liberties agenda," and full page ads have attracted as many as 500 contributions a day to the support of the ACLU.[39] Further support comes from Dr. David Hyatt, president of the National Conference of Christians and Jews. He responded to the Dallas comment by Dr. Bailey Smith on God's not hearing the prayer of a Jew by calling it "theologically primitive and a throwback to a medieval way of thinking that spawned virulent anti-Semitism and culminated in the holocaust."[40]

On the other side, however, is the fact that Jerry Falwell recently received a medal from the Jabotinsky Foundation at the hands of Prime Minister Menachem Begin of Israel "in recognition of his many years of service to Israel and to the Jewish people everywhere." Rabbi Abraham Hecht, president of the Orthodox Rabbinical Alliance of America, is quoted by *Moral Majority Report* as saying that Christian leaders like the Rev. Falwell "are men of integrity, sharing many traditional beliefs of the Jewish people and . . . values (which) have long ago been rejected out-of-hand by Schindler and his ilk."[41] The national director of the Anti-Defamation League of B'nai B'rith, Nathan Perlmutter, comments in a moderate tone, "I think that looking at the fundamentalists as a monolithic group is every bit as mischievous as viewing Jews or Catholics as a monolithic group."

One promising result from this turmoil over anti-Semitism is that evangelicals and Jews have come together under the sponsorship of the American Jewish Committee and *Christianity Today* (a major evangelical periodical) to discuss these matters. Both groups pledged to continue to work through the issues together; among them are: the conversion of Jews, the sources of anti-Semitism in evangelical theology, biblical interpretation and practice, and religious and other human rights. Many evangelicals, including some prominent Southern Baptists, have already publicly repudiated the Smith remark, such as J. William Angell of Wake Forest University, who found Smith's statements "not only untrue, unscriptural, and unkind; they are also . . . far removed from the teachings and spirit of Jesus whom he pretends to serve."[42] So distressed were many other Southern Baptists with Smith's remark that in near by Waco, Texas, a group of pastors affirmed a response prepared by Dr. James E. Wood, Jr., immediate past executive director of the Baptist Joint Committee on Public Affairs. This response was presented in the form of an affirmation of Baptist concern for the Jewish community and in the context of the High Holy Days of the Jewish calendar year. It recalls the 1972 Southern Baptist resolution repudiating anti-Semitism in all its form. On September 20, 1980, it was read at Yom Kippur services in the synagogues of Waco and in Southern Baptist churches of that city the next day. It is reproduced in the Appendix, p. 148.

In tribute to such efforts, Rabbi Marc Tanenbaum commented in a Reformed Judaism symposium on the Christian right:

> The most significant thing that happened around that episode was not his [Smith's] statement but the response to it, the thousands of letters, telegrams, and editorials from Baptist leaders, and resolutions adopted by Baptist seminaries, speaking of love for Jews, Judaism, and Israel and a condemnation of anti-Semitism.

Other groups have good reason to object to the Religious Right's insensitivity to pluralism. Racial and ethnic minorities receive little attention in the programs of the religious right. Women see themselves as being forced into limited stereotypical roles which ignore the fact that they now comprise 42% of the national workforce. The democratic process can only work in this country if it gives full voice to the many timbres of its human chorus. No single group can carry the tune for all of the nation's peoples.

To use a different image, we cannot fully "stand in someone else's shoes," even in our finest empathetic moments. Those of us who are well-to-do cannot entirely comprehend the frustrations of the poor. We cannot hope to represent the subtleties of different cultures, races, geographies, and faiths that constitute the rich variety of our national family. Therefore we count on the diversity within our political representation to sharpen our empathy and to instruct us in areas of ignorance. Imperfect though that representation may be, we benefit from plural representation of a plural society. Democracy requires us humbly to seek compromise among the competing truths from our respective viewpoints and to mediate our interests and needs within the resources available to our nation. This spirit of compromise and humility, so essential to the functioning of a democracy, is missing from the religious right, and its lack constitutes the fourth challenge.

Threat to Democracy: Passionate, Vindictive Certitude

The more certain one is that one speaks the word of God, the more likely one is to hear contrary voices as coming from the devil.

Devils are to be destroyed. One does not strike up a compromise with the devil without risking one's own salvation. When wrestling with the devil, any tactic will do. Senator George McGovern, one of the "devils" who has been wrestled to the ground, speaks of the New Right as "political theologians, priestly exorcists." He sees the suspicion, malice, and ill will generated by both the secular and religious right as a degradation of political dialogue. Senator Thomas McIntyre, also a fallen demon from rightist attacks, pleads for a restoration of the "politics of civility":

> We live in a free, open and pluralistic society, the kind of society in which issues of profound meaning to many citizens must be resolved in the public forum. We have *methods* of problem-solving, but if they are to work well we must also have a problem-solving *spirit*. One ingredient of that spirit is an understanding that solutions to real problems that are defined differently by different groups within our society will rarely, if ever, wholly square with the views of any one group.
>
> If we accept such disappointments, it is not because we are willing to abandon our own principles merely for the sake of togetherness. Rather, it is because we place a high value indeed, comparable even to the value we place on human life, on the democratic process. Speaking—proudly—as an American politician, I can testify that despite its imperfections the workings of that process call forth all the ingenuity of the human mind toward reaching accommodations that respect, *as much as possible*, all the differing values of all the differing moral systems within the community.[43]

While still in Congress and during the Panama Canal Treaty debates, Senator McIntyre addressed his colleagues in a more hard-hitting tone with these warning words about both right and left ideologues who practice a "politics of threat and vengeance":

> By proceeding from the flawed premise that all of us are alike, it is easy for ideologues to conclude that we must see every issue as they see it—unless there is something sinister in our motivation.
>
> And they proceed from that premise . . . with an arrogance born of the conviction that they and they alone have a corner on patriotism, morality, and God's own truths, that their values and standards and viewpoints are so unassailable they justify any means, however coarse and brutish, of imposing them on others.[44]

Another senator who has felt the sting of passionate certitude from the right is Mark Hatfield, himself an evangelical. In that same session on the Panama Canal Treaty, Hatfield noted three concerns about the radical right, the first being that "they want to have the American flag wrapped around their viewpoint," the third being "this horrible, cancerous disease of anti-Semitism," and:

> The second thing these individuals do is baptize their position with religious nomenclature. I have letters here, 'I thought you were a born again Christian. Now I know you are not because you support the treaty.'
>
> They do not bother to ask my view of Jesus Christ in an effort to reach some determination of my salvation: Instead, they choose to make a judgment on my religious salvation on the basis of my position regarding the Panama Canal Treaty.[45]

With this background of political testimony we can hear the calm wisdom of the Executive Committee of the National Council of Churches as it stated the citizenship responsibilities of Christians:

> The humility to see government leaders and oneself as constantly under divine judgment and mercy is a contribution to democratic political vitality and is important for opposing totalitarianism and demagoguery. . . .
>
> As citizens, Christians must not abdicate their responsibility because there is no 'pure' candidate, no absolutely correct and clear course of action. God's grace frees Christians to 'think our way to a sober estimate based on the measure of faith that God has dealt to each of us.' (Romans 12:3) Christians may not agree on all political decisions, but they are enjoined not to hold one another in contempt, for all stand before God's tribunal. In the tempering fires of political compromise and accommodation to the needs and interests of many diverse groups, there can be discerned no exclusively Christian vote,' nor can single issues pressures serve the best interests of our total society. Through a study of Scripture, the heritage of churches struggling to be faithful, and through the experiences of life which God opens, Christians are called upon to respond to the demands of the times and the promise of God.[46]

A group of major religious leaders gathered in Washington added their own word:

On theological and ethical grounds, we reject the assumption that human beings can know with absolute certainty the will of God on particular public policy issues.[47]

They buttressed their argument with the words of Reinhold Niebuhr about the sad times in Christian history which "show how human pride and spiritual arrogance rise to new heights precisely at the point where the claims of sanctity are made without due qualifications." The Washington Interreligious Staff Council echoes with: "It is arrogant to assert that one's position on a political issue is 'Christian', and that all others are 'un-Christian', 'secular humanism', 'immoral', or 'sinful'."[48]

The conservative evangelical journal *Christianity Today* agrees that there is no one position on complex social issues. While the Bible does indeed give clear principles, the editorial warns, "we must be prepared to recognize that sincere and conscientious Christians may apply these principles in different and sometimes opposite ways."[49]

In a thoughtful sermon to his United Church of Christ congregation in Gainesville, Florida, the Rev. Larry Reimer said in October, 1980:

> It just dawned on me that they (Moral Majority) are not claiming that the majority of citizens follows them. They are just claiming that they hold the majority on morality.
>
> Christianity is at its worst when it moves in this direction. H.R. Trevor Roper said, 'The most persistent heresy in Christianity is the puritan heresy, the attempt to make everyone else conform to one's own established level of purity.'[50]

Theologian Robert McAfee Brown criticizes Falwell's book *Listen, America!* for its handling of biblical exegesis, its limited sources of authority, and its sloppy use of evidence. Regarding biblical exegesis, Brown observes:

> . . . Falwell again uses sources selectively, so that partial truths go bail for the full truth. 'The sin of homosexuality,' he writes, 'is so grievous, so abominable in the sight of God, that He destroyed the cities of Sodom and Gomorrah because of this terrible sin' (p. 181).

That confident assertion leaves out a significant element of the biblical account of what happened to Sodom, as the book of Ezekiel . . . makes clear: 'Behold, this was the guilt of your sister Sodom: She and her daughters had pride, surfeit of food, and prosperous ease, but did not aid the poor and needy' (Ezekiel 16:49). The notion that destruction might come to those with a 'surfeit of food and prosperous ease' who do not 'aid the poor and needy,' never comes into Falwell's purview.[51]

Brown observes that the Bible does not even begin to compete with Milton Friedman, General Lew Walt, Senator Jesse Helms, and Brigadier General Andrew J. Gatsis as chief sources of authority for Falwell's views in his book. He further charges that the book does not come off well for giving straight facts and playing fair with the evidence, noting several examples and saying, "He uses slanted language, presents opinions as facts, grounds highly questionable assertions on the authority emanating from a Southern Baptist pulpit."[52]

Worried that the religious right had "an attractive program that is politically foolish and religiously idolatrous," the Indiana Council of Churches feared the destruction of competent and conscientious leadership in all levels of government as seen in the following newsletter:

> The premises of this religious political movement are faulty and naive. No elected official, despite personal convictions or election rhetoric, can deliver a pure report card in a democratic society such as ours; public policy evolves out of a multiplicity of forces which leads to compromise. And this new political movement is confronting that reality.
> It is religiously destructive and politically dangerous to pursue a course outlined only by the 'left', the 'right' or the 'middle'. The tactics of disruption and discrediting, without a constructive message is doomed to failure. The problem is the interim damage.[53]

When the Synod of the Mid-South convened on September 9, 1980, as a regional court for the Presbyterian Church, U.S., it expressed dismay "at the arrogance of these groups which would presume to discredit the Christian conviction and commitment of public officials because of a difference in political viewpoint." It affirmed a belief "in the perfect holiness and the complete sovereignty of God, as expressed in the first and second commandments," and declared "our confession of the reality and pervasiveness of human sinfulness prevents us from identifying any human leader, any group, any government, any political system or any party platform with the will of God or as the work of God. . . ."[54] Mecklenburg Presbytery, also of the Presbyterian Church, U.S., meeting in North Carolina said firmly:

> . . . that while it is appropriate for Christians to form organizations for political action, it is pretentious for any organization or individual to claim to have 'the' Christian, or 'the' moral, or 'the' Biblical position on any given issue.

It deplored the resorting to "half truths and intolerance," urging citizens "not to be intimidated" but to " 'test the spirits to see whether they are of God; for many false prophets have gone out into the world.' "[55]

From Union Theological Seminary in New York came a plea for making careful distinctions between the word of God and human political views. Its president said:

> Like other political systems, democracy is one way of coping with the differences that divide human beings. American democracy is unusual in its full protection of the right of religious people to say 'Thus says the Lord' to government along with the freedom of other people to say 'Not so.' At their best, evangelical Christians do not equate their political views with God's views. The distinction was never put better than by Oliver Cromwell, when he said to two contentious groups of Scotsmen, "I beseech you, by the mercies of Christ, think that you may be wrong!' Judge Learned Hand was calling for the same political virtue—humility—when he said, 'The Spirit of Liberty is the spirit that is not too sure it is right.'
>
> My major plea to my newly political evangelical friends is that they make careful distinctions between what the Christian certainties are—God's love for the world, power to rule it, and promise to redeem it—and what the proper Christian *un*certainties ought to be. If the integrity of the family is under stress in America these days, is a constitutional amendment against abortion an effective way to

combat those stresses? Was the 18th Amendment an effective way to oppose the excesses of alcohol? In a complicated, pluralistic world, questions of political effectiveness are very 'iffy.'[56]

The faculty of that same seminary, while responding to the offense of Bailey Smith's words and other polemical uses of religion in current political controversies, said that they believed "no church or religious group has an exclusive claim upon Scripture interpretation, ethical insight, or political wisdom. There is in the Christian gospel no ground for 'boasting' (Romans 3:27). In the civil covenant of our society, we expect our own insights as well as those of others to be enlarged and corrected as all appreciate the experiences of the variety of people who make up this nation and world."[57]

Even Lester Kinsolving, a religious columnist who seldom speaks harmoniously with these other voices, finds some aspects of this political activity questionable, such as when Christian Voice's leader identified Ronald Reagan as *the* Christian candidate. He finds this "as unfortunate as the so-called 'Christian Yellow pages', whose listings were confined to Born-Again Christian business establishments (which surely would have excluded all Jewish-owned carpentry shops in Nazareth)."[58] A Roman Catholic editorial made note of another irony in the following wry parenthesis: "(Were an equal number of influential Catholic clergy—assuming we had them—so blatantly political, there would be an uproar, and latent anti-Catholic bigotry would quickly surface.)"[59] Illustrating the complexity of voting, the same editorial explains:

> Let us suppose that the opposing candidates are against abortion but also against other, 'liberal' pro-life legislation for the born. It becomes difficult for a conscientious voter to choose wisely. Then the mix of religion and politics gets down to some of the terrible challenges that are the responsibility of every voter. It's time Catholics did a better job of mixing in their religious values.

Rabbi Steve Steindel, president of the Greater Pittsburgh Rabbinic Fellowship, also is concerned that "Moral Majority claims that one version of political truth is closer to God's truth. History shows great danger in such simplistic solutions." He adds that synagogues should be a source of information and a forum for political discussion, but must not be identified with a particular party or candidate.[60]

The presumption, self-righteousness, arrogance, and inflexibility of the religious right is a theme of many other documents and speeches, but it does not need further reiteration. The destructiveness to the democratic process in government has already been addressed as a concern, but the destructiveness within church institutions should also be feared. In response to the Jessup paper, which charged that the national staff was using United Methodist Church funds for repressive and totalitarian causes, the United Methodist Communications countercharged that it was Jessup and his sympathizers who were employing extremist tactics, such as:

1. A pattern of assault on institutions and their decision-making process, seeking to cut off or deny the democratic process within an institution (e.g., saying that General Conference actions only represent the opinion of general board staff).
2. Guilt by association (e.g., describing offices of radical or Marxist groups as 'next door to church agencies').
3. Refusal to debate and discuss social-political assumptions about what is happening or, in the church, their biblical and theological assumptions.
4. Innuendo and inference about persons and concerns by raising the emotional specter of supposedly 'taboo' subjects in U.S. society (use of communism and Marxism as code words).
5. A desire for the 'majority way' to be 'the only way,' thereby excluding minority viewpoints.[61]

In summary, this reply stated that only calm, objective discussion based upon facts and a search for truth and obedience would avoid divisiveness and destruction within the church.

Any danger to our democracy as a whole clearly implies a threat to all our institutions, including the church. Therefore when the religious right abuses the church, or naively allows churches to be used in pursuing political ends, it must be challenged and held accountable like any other group that seeks to undermine democratic principles.

Dangers to the Church

While granting the religious right all due participation in the political process, the religious bodies who have long been involved in politics are concerned about the political immaturity and naivete of those just entering this sphere of subtle and shrewd power relationships. Moral Majority, as was described earlier, has several entities that compose its political activity. It has educational, legislative, and legal efforts, but also a network of political action committees which work for specific candidates. Christian Voice also has political action committees such as "Christians for Reagan." This approach is markedly different from the National Council of Churches, which involves itself through its national program and its denominations in educational activities, modest lobbying, and occasional legal action, but *not* in direct support of candidates or parties. Should Christians establish Christian political action committees? Should ministers preach on behalf of particular candidates from the pulpit? While recognizing that such activities are possible in a democracy, and indeed have been carried out in other countries and by black churches in civil rights efforts in the United States, many church leaders have severe reservations and words of caution.

Southern Baptist Jimmy Allen, for example, is anxious to draw lines of self-restraint in exercising citizenship to avoid becoming a pawn of politicians or simply a political power broker:

> . . . the effort to create a religious party bloc vote is a dangerous one. In every country in which it has happened, the cause of Christ has ultimately suffered. An anti-church attitude increases. Many reject what they think is Christ for irrelevant reasons because they reject the political or economic idea of a religious leader. Dependence on political power to enforce a moral point of view can be a dangerous siren song. It leads to weakening the element of voluntary commitment. Increased dependence on political power weakens spiritual power.[62]

He says categorically that "No Baptist, even the elected leader of the Convention could claim to speak for the others. There simply has been no Baptist bloc vote. There are indeed issues of consensus in which Baptists tend to vote alike." But he notes a concern for institutional democratic process by saying:

> It is instructive also that one electronic evangelist like James Robison could be taken seriously as he claimed before a congressional committee that he knows where Southern Baptists stand on an issue like prayer in the public schools better than a denominational official like Grady Cothen who is quoting to that same committee resolutions on that subject of several consecutive conventions.[63]

He also finds politically naive the claim of the Dallas Briefing to be "non-partisan," when one political party's point of view dominated the entire event: "Calling it something else doesn't necessarily make it so. If it looks like a hen, lays eggs like a hen, and cackles like a hen, it's a hen. Calling it a cow doesn't change things."

An editorial in the magazine published by Americans United for Separation of Church and State further explicates Jimmy Allen's concern for what happens to the church from "excessive political involvement"·

> Excessive political involvement by a religious body can seriously dilute its religious or spiritual mission and turn it into just another political party, possibly subject to the laws applicable to political parties. Excessive political entanglement can create political divisions in society along religious lines, and this, the Supreme Court has warned, is one of the evils the authors of the First Amendment intended to prevent. . . . Acquisition of political power by religious bodies whets their appetite for more power. The end result of religious accretion of power is the kind of union of church and state which long typified church-state relations in Europe and elsewhere (and which drove a great many of our ancestors to these shores) and which is most visible today in Iran. . . . In any event, an overly political church will turn off great numbers of its members and offend nonmembers.[64]

Pittsburgh Presbytery executive, Rev. Harold Scott "deplores the explicit efforts of political groups to use religious organizations to further their own political processes,"[65] and Msgr. George Higgins writes, "Many Catholics, dedicated to the pro-life movement, are apparently being manipulated in the political chess game of the right wing. They are being used to support a broader 'New Right' political agenda." Higgins describes the favors and help given by the New Right political action committees as having "significantly influenced the political agenda for the right-to-life movement as a whole. So, the right wing can pin the label of pro-abortionist on candidates that it wishes to defeat for other reasons. Right-to-life groups, particularly on the local level, follow its lead. Meanwhile conservative candidates who are also pro-abortion, such as Senator John Tower, are exempt from their hit lists."[66]

President David A. Hubbard of Fuller Theological Seminary, a leading evangelical school, is careful to avoid putting evangelicals in one political camp. "For some, to be evangelical means to be conservative in politics and economics. Strident spokesmen seek to rally us around their political perspective and to recruit us in Christ's name to their economic views. For some of them, what we believe about American foreign policy, or approaches to Government spending, or the fluoridation of our drinking water is almost as important as what we believe about Christ's sacrifice or the Bible's inspiration. . . . In turn, other evangelicals have adopted more liberal political views and are seeking, often with youthful enthusiasm, to sell others on them."[67] On another occasion he comments, "I would hate for evangelical Christianity to become a spiritual version of the National Rifle Association."[68] He, too, worries about exploitation of politically naive evangelicals. The Rev. Donald Shea, Republican National Committee liaison to ethnic and religious groups, agrees that "evangelicals are not politically sophisticated and they admit they need help," so he was assigned by the Republican party to work with some 108,000 ministers in political organizing.[69]

Evangelicals for Social Action in their "Call to Responsible Christian Action" also cautioned the church:

> The gospel of Jesus Christ must not be bound in any singular political philosophy, program, party or leader. It always stands above these and judges them. Christ's lordship over all these realms, including the political, must not be limited or compromised. We therefore strongly warn against the efforts of religious leaders, however sincere

and well meaning, to affirm conservatism, liberalism, or any other political party line as distinctively and uniquely Christian. . . ."[70]

In a pastoral, almost "older brother" tone, the Oklahoma Conference of Churches (a group that has already been there politically) welcomed these groups into political action, and added:

> We would raise some words of caution, however. First, we have learned—sometimes with difficulty—to be careful about equating Christian goals with specific candidates. Issues are frequently complex and involve a mixture of good and less-than-good; but persons are always complex and ambiguous. Support of individual candidates is necessary as Christians decide which imperfect persons are most likely to further the goals they seek. Uncritical endorsement which ignores the humanity of candidates is, however, dangerously naive.[71]

When Bill Moyers took his television crew to the Dallas Briefing, he sensed a kinship with those who attended the meeting:

> I recognize deeply imprinted within me the inherited yearning for order and authority that caused them in menacing times to cleave more tenaciously to their faith. It isn't surprising that they're fighting back against the discoveries of science, decrees of government, and dilemmas of democracy that intrude upon their fixed scheme of things. . . .
>
> It is not that the evangelicals are taking politics seriously that bothers me. It is the lie they're being told by the demagogues who flatter them into believing they can achieve politically the certitude they have embraced theologically. The world doesn't work that way. There is no heaven on earth.[72]

Bill Moyers sees these good people as misled "by manipulators of politics masquerading as messengers of heaven, and their hearts will be broken by false gods who, having taken the coin of their vote or purse, will move on to work the next crowd."

Not only does political naiveté allow well-intentioned church groups to be used for the purposes of another group, but it can result in inadequate and inappropriate solutions to issues of genuine social and Christian concern. Few Christians in the United States would argue that crime among young people is *not* a problem to be addressed, or that values don't need to be taught to our youth. But is prayer in the public schools the best way to attack crime or to instill values? The Rev. John Danforth, Republican senator from Missouri, is concerned about these issues, but through his experience in politics he knows that matching specific problems to specific solutions is an arduous, chancy effort, with the distinct possibility that solutions may create more problems than they solve. He discusses prayer in the public schools:

> For those within a religious tradition, it is simply not true that one prayer is as good as any other. Prayer is related to the content of the faith, and it is the job of the churches, not the government, to describe what that content is. Any thought that the form of prayer is of no matter to denominations should be put to rest by considering the enormous controversies triggered by recent liturgical reform in the Roman Catholic and Episcopal churches.
>
> In addition to the wording of prayers, the time and place of public worship is of great concern to religious denominations. The time of worship (e.g., the Sabbath, the Day of Resurrection, days of obligation) and the place (religious art and architecture) both point to the content of the underlying faith. No denomination would be willing to delegate the organization of public worship to a school board, and it is unlikely that any worship organized by a school board would bear any relationship to religion.[73]

In the name of the *integrity of religion,* therefore, Danforth would oppose using the school system to provide a religious solution to the problem of instilling values and overcoming crime among young people.

Senator Hatfield maintains that both the credibility of the church and the identity of Christianity in a modern, complex world, are at stake in these considerations. This concern for maintaining a distinct Christian identity is at the heart of Orthodox Fr. John Meyendorff's anxiety about whatever ideological role the church may play in society and politics:

> The real danger for Christians lies not in political activity as such, but in a loss of their Christian identity. In fighting the horrors of racism,

discrimination and oppression, the liberals of the sixties were (and still are) often unaware of the danger of jumping on the bandwagon of secular revolutionary ideologies whose ultimate goal is not to protect human dignity, but to destroy it. In struggling against abortion legislation, which amounts to an even more horrible and self-righteous legal genocide of innocent human beings, the conservative Christians of today should equally be aware that their activity will lose its integrity if it is pursued in an unholy alliance with a reawakened Ku Klux Klan, or simply and naively integrated into the ideology of a 'business as usual' capitalist society. . . . The Christian faith and the values it implies will simply cease to be credible if it is reduced to political games and identified with electoral ambitions. . . .[74]

Recognizing also that the church is a human institution, with all the human tendencies toward pride and sin, the Presbyterian Church, U.S. General Assembly argued from a Protestant perspective:

The task of the church and of individual Christians in the political sphere is to serve *God,* nor ourselves: to bear witness to the God who is concerned about *all* (people), not just Christians or the church. Our goal in this sphere, therefore, can never be to win special privileges for the church and its members, or to gain control by the church over political, social and economic structures and institutions and make them subservient to the church.[75]

The possibility of the church seeking power for ecclesiastical self-service is addressed in one of John C. Bennett's principles for appropriate church state behavior in his book, *Christians and the State:*

The Churches in America should not use their members as political pressure groups to get special ecclesiastical privileges for themselves as against other religious bodies. They should not seek legislation . . . which interferes with the religious liberty of minorities and they should be thankful that the courts stand guard at this point.

No church, no matter how powerful, should bring pressure on the state to enact laws which are based upon principles that depend for their validity on its own doctrine or ethos. . . . It is wrong to seek to make the ethos of one part of the community the basis of law.[76]

Imposing the ethics of one part of the community as the basis of law for the entire national community is an attempt at an American moralism akin to civil religion, says evangelical Robert Webber.[77] He observes that Falwell, while attracting Christian followers through the Old Time Gospel Hour, is also trying to bring together in Moral Majority all who support a return to "moral America." This includes Mormons, Jews, and persons of any or no commitment. From what source are the moral standards of America derived, and who determines them? Webber is concerned that Christians make a distinction between mere civil religion and the transcending, redeeming power of Christ. He fears that Moral Majority may succumb to national self-righteousness, idolatry of the state, accommodation to questionable policies of national leaders who make of God a tribal god and Christ's salvation superfluous. Already there are many fundamentalists and evangelicals who thoroughly confuse civil religion and Christianity, Webber states.

Although none of the church leaders amply quoted in these pages has put it quite so baldly, another implicit danger to the church is the tension that stretches the bonds of Christian community when one group defines itself as "true Christians" and discards the rest. When America is "Christianized," will only conservative or fundamentalist Christians be the "real Christian" leaders? What happens to the majority of the Roman Catholic Church? Do Presbyterians, Lutherans, Episcopalians, Methodists, Baptists, and the like have a voice only if they subscribe to a highly conservative theology? Is there a particular reading of Scripture that some Pentecostalists won't pass? The church has endured inquisitions, reformations, splintering, heresy trials, and various other acts of purification, and, God willing, it shall continue to endure our loveless quarrels in the name of Love. There is always a price to be paid, whether for the lovelessness of our faith, or the faithlessness of our love. When we set ourselves up to be the judge of our own and one another's faithfulness, Christ suffers, the mission of the church suffers, and all Christians suffer.

One of the prices to be paid, says Martin Marty, is "the rise of a new anticlericalism and a new antichurchism among many now congenial people who will find their candidates and themselves crowded out."[78] As some people are already saying, if this is the way religion and politics mix, then let's get religion out of politics. For the sake of all Christian involvement in politics it is important that the religious right learn quickly the arts and graces of democracy. Otherwise the door may be slammed shut upon all religious language, argument, testimony, and other public expressions of religiously-held values. Precisely because of our belief that Christians have both a right and an obligation to translate their religious sensitivities into public citizenship, the comments and criticisms of other religious perspectives need to be heard by the Christian New Right.

Right On! What of the Future?

From this incomplete but many-dimensioned chorus of voices it is clear that even in their shared criticisms of the religious right the differences and nuances of tradition are evident. Some aspects of the Christian right are more disturbing to some groups within the ecumenical church than to others, and in some instances the silence of a religious body is as significant as what it chooses to say.

Mainline liberal Protestants, for instance, are disturbed when the religious right ignores such social and ethical problems in the society as: world hunger and poverty, the trampling of human rights in many parts of the world, the poverty and unemployment in the United States, the racism and sexism in society, the minority groups who are being overlooked, the mounting danger to peace through the arms race, the politically dangerous posturing of nations toward one another, and the new hard choices and abuses of nature which science and technology pose. They tend to see the issues raised by the Pro-Family Movement as personal and individual, not to be regulated by governmental decree. Partly because of differences in their own ranks, liberal Protestants prefer a laissez faire policy. Since they are not militantly opposed to abortion and unrestricted homosexuality, they are categorized by the religious right as *for* abortion and homosexuality, which is certainly an unfair distortion of their position. Their positions are cautiously for human rights aspects of the issues, and ambivalent and diverse otherwise. Within the ranks of mainline denominations there is also a sizeable conservative core which is becoming more assertive, adding to the complexity of any response.

Concern for religious liberty, freedom of speech, and pluralism within the society are very important to liberal white Protestants. The experience of the colonial period in this country is a reminder to them of the significance of a nonestablished, religious tradition. The Protestant wariness of Roman Catholic and Orthodox majorities in other parts of the world also reinforces their claim for separation of church and state.

Protestant black church leaders make common cause with white liberal Protestants on many social and ethical issues. However, because of concern for family morality issues and for an evangelical theology, black church leaders have some agreement with and appreciation for several of the positions promoted by groups like Moral Majority. Still, they deplore the blindness to racism and to poverty, and they are not drawn to the New Right political agenda of economic conservatism and antigovernment attitudes. But issues like "pro-choice" on abortion are not automatically supported by black leaders, who join in a deep respect for unborn human life and who fear that relaxed laws could militate against blacks. They look at abuses of sterilization and worry that loose abortion laws could be the first step down the road to another genocide. The super-patriotism of the Christian right does not resonate for black citizens, but much of the theology and religious language about decency, drugs, and values does. Support for this viewpoint is expressed in a letter to the author from Edward A. Freeman, an executive of the National Baptist Convention, U.S.A., in the Appendix, p. 147.

Although black church leaders are also concerned about religious liberty, they have practiced a mix of religion and politics which has much similarity to the political action groups within Christian Voice, Moral Majority, and others. Civil rights and socio-political-economics have been talked in black pulpits for many years, and political leaders supportive of the black community receive public notice and guidance from black churches. Bloc voting has been a means of political survival for blacks, so they can hardly take offense at the religious right's efforts to back "Christian" candidates. In a recent convocation on the black church in the eighties Dr. Gayraud Wilmore of Colgate Rochester Divinity School cautioned the black community to maintain its political independence and to be selective in its collaboration with other groups. He is concerned that blacks are the most accessible scapegoats for the New Right. An even bigger danger in his judgment is cultural annihilation. He calls for an independent black movement which is willing to work with other groups but which retains its own agenda.

White evangelicals are also in a peculiar bind. Although only the most fundamentalist among them are caught up in the pre-tribulation or post-tribulation rapture, end-times theology, they reverence the Scriptures in a similar manner and read from those Scriptures a congenial personal morality. As was noted earlier, they divide over the scope of, and appropriate position on many social issues; for example, they come down much harder on abortion than on ERA, and they are strongly for prayer in public schools. Many evangelicals continue to abhor involvement in politics, while some, like the "Sojourners" group, are oriented to utopianism rather than to conservatism. Evangelical groups like the Southern Baptists hold to a strong tradition of separation of church and state, which makes them quite uncomfortable with apparent excesses in blending religion and politics by the Christian right. There are many evangelicals among the Historic Peace Churches, which find the "strong America" militarism of the religious right directly counter to their views. Evangelicals play important compassionate roles among the poor in many denominations, and the lack of this emphasis in the religious right is disturbing to the Nazarenes and the Salvation Army, among others.

Roman Catholics, too, face some dilemma. The role of women in the Catholic church is being challenged, but the message thus far gives little hope to women who make common cause with Protestant liberals. The social issues that concern Roman Catholics are inclusive of the poor, minorities, global neighbors, ecology, and other "liberal causes." But issues related to sexual morality, and particularly the abortion question, are not very negotiable, and the Right-to-Life movement has strong Roman Catholic participation. Theologically they are not very compatible with fundamentalism, but on the Pro-Family issues they tend to share similar views. Roman Catholics also agree with the protection of parochial schools and other issues of taxation that are advocated by Jerry Falwell and Earl Little of the Christian Legal Defense and Education Foundation. The separation of church and state is historically less clear cut for Catholics than for Protestants. Roman Catholicism is also characterized by waves of immigration, and today those waves are strongly Hispanic. These immigrants are often poor, but eager to establish a place in the American dream. They bring a new energy, as yet not well defined politically, to the society. Exactly how the Roman Catholic Church intends to channel this political energy is unclear. On the one hand the Pope recently withdrew priests from public office (for example, Father Drinan from the United States Congress), while on the other, Cardinal Madeiros has called upon his parishioners to vote for candidates on the basis of their stand on abortion. What is clear is that a sizeable number of Moral Majority members are drawn from the Catholic ranks. So far it seems that the Catholic Church in the United States, and generally the Orthodox Church as well, hold a firm middle ground position and choose to avoid a confrontation with the religious right.

Jews, however, have an even more delicate balance to maintain. Fully aware of the anti-Semitism that has emanated from fundamentalist pulpits and radio in the past, American Jews are alert to potential expressions of anti-Semitism today. A fundamentalist reading of Revelation requires the Jews to be gathered in Israel before the Second Coming, so Israel is supported for "theologically self-serving" reasons the Jews can hardly applaud. It is difficult, on the one hand, to encourage the pro-Israel stance of the religious right while, on the other, firmly rejecting their "Christian America" goal as a threat to religious liberty. The "moral agenda" of the Christian right is not the agenda of the Jews, but neither are Jews comfortable with all the stands of Roman Catholicism, black church affirmative action, and National Council of Churches positions on the Middle East. The Jews are passionate defenders of religious and civil liberties, and they will work with many diverse groups in support of human rights for all. But, like other religious bodies, they contain within their own family many different viewpoints on issues and strategies.

Of course, diversity within the ranks is not alien to conservatives and the New Right, either. Some important differences were consciously held at arms length until after Ronald Reagan was elected. The enthusiasm for moral legislation that traditionalists share is not necessarily the first order of business for libertarian conservatives, who want government restraints on business reduced. James Wall, using William Safire's clumsy terms "Tradright" and "Libright," predicts:

> . . . the conservative split will really begin to show when some of the Moral Majority-backed members of Congress introduce legislation to offer as government standard the 'moral principles' of Christian fundamentalists. Librightists will be fighting against governmental restrictions on safety codes, clean-air standards, and environmental impact statements, but they will be embarrassed when Tradright conservatives insist that while the government should leave us alone in business practice, it needs to get involved in regulating sexual practices.[1]

He also sees issues of free speech, Israel, and a "pre-tribulation Rapture" anti-intellectualism as sources of uneasy division within conservatism. Some politicians, like William Sweeney of the Democratic Congressional Campaign Committee, expect the religious right to become disenchanted quickly: "I give them six months before they start attacking Reagan."[2] Other observers note that funds for political action are not as plentiful as the religious right anticipated. According to *Church and State,* November, 1980, the political action arm of Moral Majority reported receipts of only $22,089 and is now inactive. It also says Christian Voice in February had projected a million dollar budget, but that it had reported receipts of only $122,000 through July.

Election analyses since November 1980 are also urging that the role of the religious right not be overstated. Michigan's Survey Research Center produced a study based upon 10,000 interviews, leading study director Arthur Miller to believe that fundamentalist impact on the election has been much exaggerated. The New York Times/CBS election-day poll of voters found that a slightly smaller percentage of born-again white Protestants (61%) than of other white Protestants (63%) actually voted for Reagan. Seymour Martin Lipset and Earl Raab note that the decline in the vote of five senators targeted by the National Conservative Political Action Committee (and the religious right) was almost identical with that of the Democratic senatorial candidates in eighteen non-targeted states in the North. Also, of the NCPAC officially endorsed House candidates in 103 contests, 57 lost, compared to 46 who were elected, a result closely parallel to the party distribution for all 435 House seats. The testimony of several winning candidates that they were not helped by the support of the religious and New Right, and the opinion poll research which questions whether losing candidates were on balance actually damaged by their support are additionally persuasive to Lipset and Raab.[3]

Before those who oppose the program of the religious right begin to gloat at the potential for their being swept aside now that the power is in conservative hands, it is important to remember who these people are. Coming out of a sense of alienation, of marginality, they are giving vent to frustration, anger, and moral outrage through an acceptable political process. Despite their tendency to see government leaders as devils or powers of evil and darkness, they are giving democracy a try and have had some real success. Still, they are quite prone to Edward Shils' portrait of extremism:

> Ideological extremists . . . because of their isolation from the world, feel menaced by unknown dangers. The paranoiac tendencies which are closely associated with their apocalyptic and aggressive outlook make them think that the ordinary world, from which their devotion to the ideal cuts them off, is not normal at all; they think it is a realm of secret machinations. . . . Their image of the 'world' as the realm of evil, against which they must defend themselves and which they must ultimately conquer, forces them to think of their enemy's knowledge as secret knowledge.[4]

A Christianity which exaggerates the evil of the world, neglecting God as creator of a good creation, falls prey to other exaggerations also. Sinfulness is so condemned that salvation, about which much is said, loses its joy in the anger of judgment. A rigid sense of what is pure and right increasingly limits the number of persons who are "acceptably" saved. Pride easily dominates when one adopts a stern authoritarian position that knows itself to be pure in judgment and action. Christianity has many rich and subtle facets to its theology, but when certain aspects of the faith are allowed to dominate and obscure others, an unhealthy distortion occurs. Concentration upon the end of the world makes only too bearable the injustices and hardships of the present, while pre-tribulation rapture theology smugly says, "The Great Tribulation will strike the wicked, but as a child of God, it will never touch you."[5] Either aloof alienation or aggressive action are the likely responses of the evangelical fundamentalist to the political scene. That the Christian right has chosen to assert itself in the political swim could be healthy, unless that participation is subverted, or manipulated and then ignored.

One interesting way to look at the "ethical maturity" of the religious right's political life is to see how they measure up to the standards set by Donald Shriver and Karl Ostrom in their book, *Is There Hope for the City?*[6] Shriver and Ostrom found, in their extensive study of the Raleigh, Durham, Chapel Hill area of North Carolina, four characteristics of ethical maturity, the absence of any one of which leads to imbalance and exaggeration in political life. They are: (1) a sense of "basic trust," (2) a high level of integrity between what one believes and the actions one takes, (3) openness to other points of view and to people quite different from oneself, and (4) public regard, in which one is willing to sacrifice self for the public good. The religious radical rightist, indeed extreme leftists, too, may be very strong in at least two of these characteristics, but weak in the other two. A high level of integrity between what one believes and how one acts and a willingness to sacrifice for the public good are two characteristics of many rightists, and religion reinforces these two characteristics. But a lack of basic trust in the world, the society, and the institutions of that society, makes activism and sacrifice serve some strange purposes. Also a lack of openness to people with differing points of view, backgrounds, religious perspectives, race, or ideology may strongly limit the size of the public for which they are willing to sacrifice.

The bid for political participation by the religious right is an opportunity for them to develop some basic trust in the society which they help to govern. It is also an opportunity to be required to confront other sectors of the public with whom they have had little association. If they are treated with respect, perhaps their ability to respect others will expand.

The alternative is grim. Our society already has its share of vigilantes and socially apathetic dropouts. The U.S. Justice Department's Community Relations Service reports 336 serious racial incidents for the first half of fiscal year 1980, 38 more than all of 1979. It expected the number to double by the end of that current fiscal year. Also, it reports a 225% increase in cases associated with Indo-Chinese, a 189% increase in Ku Klux Klan cases, and a 142% increase in police use of excessive force cases. In reflecting upon the difference between the Miami riot of 1980 and the riots of the sixties, the Justice Department says that the Miami black rioters, many of them Vietnam trained, have demonstrated that they are no longer afraid of police officers, no longer adherents to non-violence or trustful of national black leaders like Andrew Young. Although there were less fatalities in Miami than in Newark, Detroit, or Watts in the 1960's, the level of terrorism and violence was more vicious and deliberate. Black leaders understand it as an expression of pent-up frustration with social systems and institutions that have failed to respond to the urgency signalled in the '60s.[7]

From Nathan Perlmutter, director of the Anti-Defamation League of B'nai B'rith, come reports of clandestine military exercises for paramilitary units of the KKK. He characterizes the participants as "armed racists and pathological haters of blacks, Jews and other minority groups." He says, "A clear danger of new Klan violence is more serious than ever before."[8] Black leaders are only too aware of an increase in violent, anti-black activity by groups like KKK, and some of them fear a national conspiracy. They mention the murder of at least 25 black children in Atlanta; the senseless gunning down of a black teen-aged girl in Youngstown, Ohio; several ugly killings in Buffalo, New York, in which the hearts of two black taxi drivers were cut out; the Greensboro, North Carolina, anti-Klan march; and the attack upon Vernon Jordan. Jesse Jackson, leader of Operation PUSH, says, "Blacks correlate events in Buffalo, Atlanta and other cities with the events in government, such as Reagan opening up his campaign talking about state's rights and minority rule in South Africa, and the right-wing element in the church. . . . Racism has become fashionable again and feelings of guilt toward blacks have turned to feelings of hostility."[9] Not all black leaders see persuasive evidence for a conspiracy, but they sense a climate in which such fears grow.

Anti-Semitism is perceived to be on the increase, too, according to various leading Jews, such as Rabbi Schindler, who reports:

> Whatever the reasons, anti-Semitism is alive and kicking in this land. The number of reported incidents mounts daily. Synagogues are defaced, cemeteries desecrated, religious schools vandalized, slanderous leaflets are distributed, threatening telephone calls are made, and individuals have been pelted with rocks. So far there has been only property damage, and some minor injuries, no deaths, so far, thank God, in North America. . . .
>
> . . . the respite which we have had since World War II has come to its end. The memory of the holocaust is fading. The sense of guilt has waned. Hatred of the Jews is stirring once again, and we had best be ready.[10]

Anti-black, anti-Semitic, often anti-Catholic, the Klan is predominantly a Protestant organization which looks upon the Protestant church as "one of our greatest allies," claims Imperial Wizard Wilkinson. The Klan looks for emotional issues that appeal to conservatives and sides with them, whether or not their support is sought. They have made their presence felt on such religious right subjects as abortion, homosexuality, the ERA, prayer in public schools, national defense, immigration, and foreign aid. C.W. Ward, black pastor of First Baptist Church in Raleigh, North Carolina, says, "Something greater than the Klan disturbs me, and that is the whole wave of ultra-conservatism that is sweeping the country. It has created a climate that may allow the Klan to thrive."[11] By this he does not imply that Christian right activists are Klan members, but only that their own militance encourages the Klan, because they take similar positions on a number of issues. If, however, the religious right feels itself politically betrayed by more traditional conservative groups, the possibility for further alliance with violent groups like the Klan certainly exists.

A Personal Prescriptive Postscript

In these concluding pages the author chooses to peel off the protective cover of research documentation and the quotation of other points of view. Although personal viewpoint is always expressed through the selection and organization of material, it is fair at some point to come forward with biases fullblown. These are the views of the author and should not be construed as official statements for any of the organizations or agencies with which she has various affiliations and responsibilities. The views have to do with what we learn and what we do in relation to politics and also in relation to the realm of the spirit.

A Political Word

Groups quoted in this book have already agreed thoroughly that all sorts of Christians ought to be involved in politics, and that the frustration of political participation by fundamentalists of the right might well have disastrous effects upon the body politic. However, not much has been said about the apathy and political ineffectiveness of moderate and liberal Christians. Christians who were actively involved in the civil rights era and in the national debate over Vietnam have somewhat mysteriously spent themselves. The war in Vietnam *was* ended—a major turnaround; and the loss of national will for war was an important factor in that remarkable shift away from the use of a nation's ultimate arsenal. Although it did not happen soon enough to suit many of us, and though our country was not as magnanimous in the restoration of peace as some would have liked, and though the continued political instability and aggressive militarism of Southeast Asia has given no one cause for rejoicing, still, our country did finally extricate itself from grievous uses of its power. Why have those who disengaged themselves from "the establishment" in those years refused in such great numbers to accept a responsible role in it again?

Similarly, the civil rights period did result in some significant legislation. It is true that many whites felt that the "black is beautiful" independence movement was a repudiation of their participation, but other whites did understand that blacks needed to lead their own liberation in order to be truly "liberated." It is also true that legislation is just the *beginning* of the struggle to overcome racism, especially in the sphere of economics. But that is not a reason for withdrawal from political action—it is a reason for increasing one's involvement. Some blacks charge that some of the energy once directed toward combatting racism is now taken up in fighting sexism. Whether or not that is true, one must confess that the forces mobilized in the sixties have not been mustered as we enter the eighties. This is especially tragic because unemployment for black young people has become destructively high and the rise of KKK-type racial violence is alarming.

Low political involvement and a splintering of old coalitions that had proved effective in the sixties (so much so that the New Right copied the practice of single-issue groups forming coalitions) have taken their toll in this election. We are reminded that only 26% of eligible adult voters elected Ronald Reagan—hardly an avalanche. Furthermore, as political analyst Greg Denier claims, if 167,214 voters had swung the other way, all four liberal senators whose defeat had been targeted by the New Right would have stayed in office.[1] Denier also argues that Reagan won by successfully shedding his image as an extreme rightist, while Carter lost in part over rejection of policies which were far from liberal. This suggests that we have misperceived the 1980 election as a "massive turning to the right." We will make a huge mistake if we conclude from the 1980 election that there is no hope for a progressive Christian role in politics, especially since so many of the troops have been inactive.

Good sense would seem to suggest that new efforts should be made to form new coalitions. Some examples are already beginning to shape, like People for the American Way, which, according to one of its members, has brought together a "group of religious, business, media and labor leaders to 'reaffirm the traditional American values embodied in the Constitution of freedom of religion, belief, thought and expression.' People for the American Way plans to use the mass media—TV, radio, print—to present a positive message of respect for diversity, pluralism and tolerance to counter the 'divisive and anti-democratic' message of the religious new right." Perhaps the election will serve to reinvigorate those who had been lethargically debating whether or not involvement in politics really matters. A second suggestion is that the party system of politics be given renewed support. In a time when the possibility of a "Christian party" is being considered (something like the Rev. Ezra Stiles Ely's efforts in the 1820's), Christians who think such actions are hazardous to religious liberty should help restore the vigor of our weak political party system. This means trying to get evangelicals of the right to work within the party system, too. As individual citizens, each of us should find an appropriate party "home," while at the same time avoiding the tendency to bring party politics into our church organizations. Liberals who find the Democratic, Republican, or other parties too "impure" for their enlarged and enlightened vision of the world are acting like pre-Moral Majority fundamentalists!

A Word for the Spirit

Perhaps even more presumptive than giving political advice is an attempt to speak a spiritual word, but in some ways the crisis of our times is more spiritual than political. In the conviction that each of us has something to contribute to one another, these observations and confessions are offered by one Presbyterian ecumenical Christian, with liberal Christians particularly in mind:

The liberal desire not to impose one's own religious views on anyone else is admirable, but if too rigorously followed it leads to an "unGodly silence." We must be free to speak the truth that is in us, or religious liberty is a muzzle rather than a protection. In the name of not offending others whose doctrine and biblical interpretation may differ, we tend toward minimal use of language about God,

Christ, the Holy Spirit, salvation, or Scripture. Unwittingly the sources of our spiritual energy are diminished when we do not allow the force of utterance to clarify our motives and spur our hopes into action. We do not have to spice our every thought with "Praise the Lord," but there are times when the Lord must be praised in order for our deeds to be put into some perspective and our faith to be replenished. Let us not be afraid in our various ecumenical coalitions to speak words of hope and strength to one another freely, and let us make clear to each other that our hope and strength come from God!

At the same time, we need not apologize for joining in the father's cry to Jesus over his sick child, "I believe; help my unbelief!" Some of the most poignantly and profoundly enriching biblical narratives describe the agony of the search for faith. Christians live, like Job, under the spiritual discipline of incomplete answers from God "whose knowledge is too wonderful for us." With Moses we plead to God, "show us your glory." We desire to know God's ways and to receive favor, but along with Moses we do not see God's face. Paul assures us, "Faith comes from what is heard, and what is heard comes by the preaching of Christ." (Romans 10:17) Through God's mercy in Christ, God "helps our unbelief," but Paul urges us, "Do not become proud, but stand in awe." (Romans 11:20) One of the spiritual strengths of liberalism at its best is the humility of acknowledging it does *not* have all the answers. It is therefore less prone to judging others harshly than are groups who have religious certainty.

There are spiritual traps, however, even in our attempts to be open and accepting of one another, so that we will "live in harmony with one another, in accord with Christ Jesus." In our eagerness to include everyone in our circle, we adamantly exclude those who are not willing to include everyone. We fail to see the contradiction in our so-called inclusive liberalism. We open the door for homosexuals, but make those who raise questions about the acceptability of homosexuality so uncomfortable that they leave. We abhor sexism and racism, and screen out those whose abhorrence does not take the same political shape or fervor as our own, thus limiting the possibility of influencing their thinking or our own. If we are socialist in leaning, we are as selective as the Moral Majority in determining who are the "true Christians." Although we have lists of "code words" for others, we employ a vocabulary that often sets up high hurdles that the uninitiated must jump, not only to agree with us but even to comprehend us.

Our desire to be inclusive is a commendable response to "Love thy neighbor as thyself," when we translate "neighbor" as surprisingly and stringently as Christ does in the parable of the Good Samaritan. A helpful spiritual exercise for the post-1980 election blues is to ask ourselves "Whom have we passed by on the other side?" Some of us would reply that the frustrated, marginal people who respond to Moral Majority are people we have ignored or discounted. It may be our parents, whose morality is still "in the Dark Ages" in the eyes of some of us. It may even be people we count as colleagues, but to whom we have failed to listen very seriously. Reestablishing communication with people who differ with us on a variety of issues, theologies, and ideologies is an important spiritual priority for religious groups in the years ahead.

The results of such enlarged communication could be humbling for people on both sides of the gulf. One hope for the religious right's involvement in politics is that it will rub shoulders with other viewpoints and become less arrogant. Perhaps liberal Christians will also become less arrogant if contact with evangelicals improves. We have eagerly delved into complex problems of economics and have fought against complacency about problems like world hunger, poverty, war, and racial prejudice. But we have only recently, through the window of feminism, taken a hard look at pornography, and we have folded our hands over the increased divorce rate, the dissolution of commitment in sexual relationships, and the destructiveness of drugs. As one pastor said in his sermon, "We have accepted as almost inevitable that public and private morality are on the slide." Have we *nothing* to say on these subjects? If it is not repressive to urge a lifestyle that diminishes world hunger, why is it necessarily repressive to urge a lifestyle that diminishes drug or sexual abuse? We have said some words of compassion where Moral Majority only voices judgment, but perhaps there are some words of judgment that we have failed to say, and for which we are answerable.

Finally, we need to rejoice, without apology, in the power and potential of things we bring to the Christian church. We have listened to some people who have been neglected by the society at large—Native Americans, Third World peoples, minorities within our own country, women, the poor. They have had a profound effect upon our thinking, and we can be deeply grateful for their taking the patient trouble to instruct us in what it is like to be aliens in their own land, to be pawns of big powers, to be forever outvoted and overlooked, to be dismissed or not taken seriously because of their sex, to be in a world of plenty but with empty pockets. Our task is to make their voices more effectively heard, so that their patience in tutoring us will result in benefit to the whole society. Again, the job is barely underway. If we simply join them on the margins of society, we will have gained them nothing. Having been entrusted with some of the burden of their anxieties, we must assist the whole church and our national and world neighbors to carry that burden, too, until it is no longer necessary. If we are to be true to them, true to our own convictions about what it is to "do justice and love mercy," and true to our understanding of Christian citizenship and discipleship, we will become more politically alive and spiritually rooted. Then we, too, are assured that what we do can make a difference. And we will.

APPENDIX

The Citizenship Responsibilities of Christians

Executive Committee Statement, National Council of Churches, September 12, 1980*

Periodically U.S. citizens have the opportunity to choose their presidential leadership and thereby the direction their nation will take into the future. As an organization whose member churches care deeply about issues which affect the quality of life of all people, the National Council of the Churches of Christ in the U.S.A. again this year presented to the Platform Committees of the Democratic and Republican national conventions a statement setting forth its views on major issues.

This year, in the midst of a political campaign during which much is being said about the "role" of Christians in politics, the National Council of Churches believes it is appropriate to state its views about the citizenship responsibilities of Christians consistent with its thirty-year history of a biblically motivated search for justice, peace, reconciliation and the succouring of the world's poor and oppressed.

In some parts of the world to declare oneself a Christian is to become politically suspect. U.S. Christians can rejoice that this is not true in the United States. The U.S. does not demand political conformity along religious or ideological lines, a heritage of religious and civil liberty to be treasured.

*Major portions of this statement were also used by the Board of Directors, Greater Dallas Community of Churches, meeting October 23, 1980 in Dallas, Texas.

Christians have obligations of citizenship to fulfill, particularly the right and duty to vote, as well as the Biblical injunction to work toward a social vision of compassion, justice, and peace. God intends for Christians to pursue the "things that make for peace and build up the common life," which would include participation in the political process.

The immense resources of Christ's grace supply the courage and inward renewal to undertake citizenship responsibilities today and in the age to come. The humility to see government leaders and oneself as constantly under divine judgment and mercy is a contribution to democratic political vitality and is important for opposing totalitarianism and demagoguery.

Above all, Christians are to love the Lord their God and their neighbor as themselves. They are to work diligently for peace, for the survival and preservation of God's creation, and for the good of all humanity. Loving one's neighbor has no boundaries of race, class, sex, or nationality, as Christ's ministry amply demonstrates. Christians are obliged to address the needs of those who may be excluded from the benefits of society or from the political process and to whom harm is being done at home or abroad.

As citizens, Christians must not abdicate their responsibility because there is no "pure" candidate, no absolutely correct and clear course of action. God's grace frees Christians to "think our way to a sober estimate based on the measure of faith that God has dealt to each of us." (Romans 12:3). Christians may not agree on all political decisions, but they are enjoined not to hold one another in contempt, for all stand before God's tribunal. In the tempering fires of political compromise and accommodations to the needs and interests of many diverse groups, there can be discerned no exclusively "Christian vote," nor can single issue pressures serve the best interests of our total society. Through a study of Scripture, the heritage of churches struggling to be faithful, and through the experiences of life which God opens, Christians are called upon to respond to the demands of the times and the promises of God.

The Advocacy Ministry of Government Liaison Offices of National Religious Organizations

Statement, Washington Interreligious Staff Council, April, 1980

The Washington Interreligious Staff Council is an organization of Washington-based government liaison offices representing national religious organizations. These include large organizations which number millions of members, and other smaller groups. Cooperative work through the Washington Interreligious Staff Council is based on a mutual respect for the faith, worship, and traditions of those serving in ministry in the nation's capital.

As members of WISC, we, the undersigned, work individually and corporately in what we believe is a ministry for peace, social justice and the common good. We experience God's presence in Washington, believe that the governmental process can serve God's purpose in the world, and choose to relate to that process on the basis of these convictions. We accept the fact that there are disagreements on how best to serve God and humankind; at the same time, we do not believe that such a fact gives any group the moral right to attack the sincerity of another's faith or commitment to justice. During the week when the "Washington for Jesus" campaign will intensify its activities in the Capital, we feel compelled, as representatives of national religious organizations, to express our understanding of the nature of the work of advocacy which our organizations undertake. Further, we wish to share our concerns about certain aspects of the "Washington for Jesus" movement and other similar efforts which we feel may uncritically and even destructively confuse issues of religion and politics.

The government is to make no decisions regarding the validity or orthodoxy of any doctrine, recognizing that it is the province of religious groups to state their doctrines, determine their politics, train their leaders, conduct worship and carry on their mission and ministries without undue interference from or entanglement with government. Yet faith groups and government work together for the maintenance of good order, the protection and extension of civil rights, the establishment of social justice and equality of opportunity, the promotion of international accord, the promotion of the general welfare and the advancement of the dignity of all persons.

An important and integral part of the ministry of religious groups is being advocates of justice for participants in the social order. God is active in both the spiritual and the civil dimensions of life. In the latter sphere, justice is enhanced by all persons of good will working together for the common good. Thus it is unnecessary and wrong for any religious group or individual to seek to "Christianize" the government or to label political views of members of Congress as "Christian" or "religious." It is arrogant to assert that one's position on a political issue is "Christian," and that all others are "un-Christian," "secular humanist," "immoral," or "sinful." There is no "Christian" vote or legislation.

Even within the Christian community describing one group's political position as "the Christian vote" and one movement's political agenda as a movement "for Jesus" is wrongly judgmental. It is also an affront to Jewish and other religious advocates whose religions hold social justice as a social form of love of neighbor. Devout Christians and Jews agree and disagree with one another and with persons of other religious faiths as well as with those outside of the religious community as such. We each bring to the political process our best and most sensitive ethical judgment, informed by our own religious traditions.

Our political activity arises from the variety of our religious traditions and experiences. We reject any attempt to judge each other's stands on particular public policy issues as moral or immoral, religious or sinful. The undersigned members of WISC express firm disagreement with individuals or coalitions who plan political action under any guise of religious worship or revivalism. We strongly oppose the exclusive use of "religious grounds" as the yardstick for determining the quality of candidates for political office. We support pluralism and freedom of all people in the United States political process. Pushing for total agreement on moral issues is *not* the same as advocating for legislation which will enhance the common good.

This statement is one of explicit disagreement with any individual or group claiming that their position on legislation is of God and that other groups or individuals differing from or voting against them are secular humanists or anti-God. This can be applied to specific issues such as the White House Conference on Families, prayer in the public schools, capital punishment, freedom of choice regarding abortion, SALT II, Panama Canal Treaties, Equal Rights Amendment, welfare, D.C. voting rights, gun control and foreign aid.

While this letter is issued during the "Washington for Jesus" gathering, our concerns extend to all situations where religion and politics are uncritically equated. The organizations we represent have and will continue to work for social justice and to share with Congress and others in government concerns and insights on current issues—while respecting the diversity and the contribution of various traditions within the United States. The undersigned look forward to this continuing interaction as we work together for peace and justice in the world. We look forward to a mutual exploration among religiously oriented people of many different viewpoints and the expectation that divine guidance can lead us all to a better appreciation of the roles we should be playing at this critical juncture in human history.

Christian Theological Observations on the Religious Right Movement

October 21, 1980

The emergence of a politically active movement popularly called "the religious right" claiming to represent "the moral majority" or "the Christian voice" has prompted us, a group representing a broad range of traditions and viewpoints in the U.S. Christian community, to issue this statement.

We disagree with many of the political positions of those in the religious right, but Christians in this country have traditionally disagreed on many political issues. A common faith does not necessarily produce a political consensus.

Our intent in this statement is not to argue for one ideological stance over against another, but to make some theological observations about certain things now being said and done in the name of Christian morality.

We want to register our agreement with some things we hear these companions in the U.S. Christian community saying. We agree that:

—Christians ought to be actively engaged in politics and influenced in their political judgments by their faith in God and loyalty to God's cause.

—Church bodies and other groups of Christians have both the right and the responsibility to make their views known on public policy issues.

—Religious leaders have both the right and the responsibility to proclaim the Word of God as they understand it in light of political realities and to interpret political realities in light of the Word of God.

—It is proper for religious bodies or organizations to provide their members and the general public with analyses of political issues and information on the voting records of office holders, and to mobilize their members in support of or in opposition to particular legislation.

We express these agreements because many criticisms of the religious right reflect what we judge to be misunderstanding of the role of the Christian community in the common life and the meaning of the constitutional principle of separation of church and state. Christians and Christian groups—whether they be ideologically on the right, the left, or in the center—have every right to seek to influence public affairs.

Nevertheless, apart from any political differences we may have with the religious right, we have strong theological objections to some of their positions and tactics.

1. On theological and ethical grounds, we object to the list of issues which the religious right has identified as the moral agenda

facing our nation. We do not simply disagree with their stance on particular items on their agenda; we find their selection of issues to be theologically and ethically inadequate. An agenda identified by Christian believers ought to reflect God's concern for the whole world. It ought to be consonant with what God has revealed of Himself through the prophets and Jesus. It ought to be faithful to what Jesus called the "weightier matters of the law." Our study of the biblical witness convinces us that the God of the prophets and of Jesus calls the people of God to work for peace and things that make for peace, to seek justice for the poor, and to care for the created order. What God wills for our common life is at heart a theological question. We regard the theology of the religious right, expressed in their choice of issues for Christian concern, as unfaithful to the fullness of biblical witness.

2. On theological and ethical grounds, we object to the moral criteria that many in the religious right use to evaluate candidates for public office. It is quite appropriate, even morally mandatory, for citizens to choose among candidates for public office in light of their stances on the great public issues of the day. But simple human decency and fairness to the candidates, concern for the common good, and most of all loyalty to the God of biblical faith surely demand that the instrument by which Christians measure candidates for public office be adequate to the task. We believe the narrow range of issues selected by such groups as the Christian Voice and the Christian Voters' Victory Fund for the purpose of rating members of Congress represents ideological preferences rather than the breadth of responsible Christian positions.

3. On theological and ethical grounds, we reject the assumption that human beings can know with absolute certainty the will of God on particular public policy issues. Many in the religious right seem to have forgotten the clear biblical witness and central Christian acknowledgment that all of us are finite, fallible, and sinful. They make claims to knowledge of God's will for our nation that no Christian is entitled to make. God wills peace, justice, and liberation for all His children. God works in history to fashion a just, participatory, and sustainable society. And the requirements of God are clear: We are to love God with all that we are; we are to love our neighbors as ourselves; we are to do justice, love mercy,

and walk humbly with our God. But we who are finite and fallible cannot claim to know with certainty the appropriate response to God's requirements at a particular moment in history. We recall and urge others to recall the wisdom of Reinhold Niebuhr:

> The sorry annals of Christian fanaticism, of unholy religious hatreds, of sinful ambitions hiding behind the cloak of religious sanctity, of political power impulses compounded with pretensions of devotion to God, offer the most irrefutable proof of the error in every Christian doctrine and every interpretation of the Christian experience which claim that grace can remove the final contradiction between man and God. The sad experiences of Christian history show how human pride and spiritual arrogance rise to new heights precisely at the point where the claims of sanctity are made without due qualifications.

4. Finally, on theological and ethical grounds, we reject the manner in which some in the religious right are engaging in political activity. There is no place in a Christian manner of political life for arrogance, manipulation, subterfuge, or holding others in contempt. There is no justification in a pluralistic and democratic society for demands for conformity along religious or ideological lines. St. Paul urges Christians to "let your manner of life be worthy of the gospel of Christ." This applies to political as well as to other forms of social life. All of us stand constantly under divine judgment and mercy. Sensitivity to this common human situation should be reflected in every Christian's political manner of life.

Bishop James M. Ault
Secretary of the Council of Bishops
United Methodist Church

Rev. Charles V. Bergstrom
Executive Director
Office for Governmental Affairs
Lutheran Council in the U.S.A.

Rev. Robert C. Campbell
Executive Secretary
American Baptist Churches in the
 U.S.A.

Ruth A. Daugherty
President
Women's Division
Board of Global Ministries
United Methodist Church

Dr. Milton B. Engebretson
President
Evangelical Covenant Church in America

Dr. John S. Groenfeldt
President
Moravian Church
Northern Province

Bishop Nathaniel L. Linsey
Christian Methodist Episcopal
  Church

Rev. C.J. Malloy, Jr.
General Secretary
Progressive National Baptist Con-
  vention, Inc.

Dorothea C. Morse
Clerk
Friends General Conference

Dr. Robert W. Neff
General Secretary
Church of the Brethren

Rev. Avery Post
President
United Church of Christ

Dr. Porter W. Routh
Interim Executive Director
Baptist Joint Committee on Public
  Affairs

Rev. Kenneth L. Teegarden
President
Christian Church (Disciples of
  Christ)

Rev. George B. Telford, Jr.
Director
Division of Corporate and Social
  Mission
Presbyterian Church in the U.S.A.

William P. Thompson
Stated Clerk
United Presbyterian Church in the
  U.S.A.

A Pastoral Letter from the Bishops, October 8, 1980

As bishops of the Episcopal Church meeting in the early autumn of an election year in the United States, we wish to speak of Christian responsibility in exercising the right to vote. In focusing on a national issue we are mindful of our brothers and sisters of this Church whose citizenship is in other countries. We hope that what we say will be of relevance and stimulation to them. We hold them in our prayers and ask for theirs in our forthcoming national decision-making.

Two matters concern us chiefly. Both represent extremes of religious response to the problems of political choice.

I. Our first concern is apathy. Hardly half the American people entitled to vote do so. For Christians, this withdrawal from political responsibility is faithless and immoral. To fail to vote or to be uninformed in voting is a denial of the biblical faith that Jesus Christ is Lord: the Lord of politics, economics, education, and social systems, as well as of our personal and family lives.

Christians are not relieved of political decision-making just because political choices involve fallible candidates—or because political choices must face debatable positions and points of view. To think so and act so betrays a hands-off-the-world assumption about God and his Christ which Scripture denies. Our God of the Old Testament is a political intervener because the cosmos he commands is moral at the core. No earthly sovereignty can violate that morality and endure. However, as Scripture declares, "If a king judges the poor with equity his throne will be established forever" (Proverbs 29:14). In the New Testament, God's intervention takes the form of a self-offering in crucifixion for the very life of the world.

Political withdrawal by Christians creates a vacuum that invites the tyranny of those who would use power for discrimination, oppression, and economic barbarism. That is the immorality of political apathy.

But it is not enough simply to vote. We urge *informed* voting, making choices on the grounds of a first principle that is biblical and basic to Christian conviction. This first principle is the sacredness of human life. From it other guideposts rise for our decision-making, all of them anchored in Scripture.

Since we hold that human life is sacred, our political choices need to reflect the best judgment we can make as to the people and platforms that honor all persons—that respond to the needs of the aged, the unemployed and the disadvantaged—that uphold racial and sexual equality—and that resist irresponsible and indiscriminate abortion as a heedless, casual birth control option.

Our political choices also need to reflect a moral resolve that American economic structures reduce the extremities of arrogant wealth and gross poverty which mark doomed societies. Callous biblical kingdoms were brought low by God's wrath. Contemporary societies are likewise under judgment for greed and indifference to human need. "What do you mean by crushing my people, by grinding the face of the poor? says the Lord God of hosts" (Isaiah 3:15).

A further imperative that flows from the sacredness of human life is Christ's call that his disciples be peacemakers. Wherever possible, our voting needs to call to account the iniquity of a runaway arms capability that supplies small nations with lethal weaponry, much of it American. Our political action must deplore the daily and deadly addition that America makes to the absurd stockpile of nuclear warheads. We now have atomic megatons adequate to kill everybody in the Soviet Union twenty times over.

Since nuclear armaments here and in the Soviet Union have created a world in which the whole can nowhere be protected against its parts, our own national security has reached the zero point. The issue is no longer the survival of one nation against another. We stand now in mortal danger of global human incineration. A computer error could trigger mutually assured destruction. American responsibility for the world beyond us compels a moral outcry against the arms race.

As a way of moving us all from apathy and toward responsibility, we have offered biblical guideposts to political decision-making. It is to be expected that we will disagree on candidates and political direction. Disagreement expresses both our freedom and the ambiguity of all choices made by sinful people in a fallen world. But at a deeper level of truth, political involvement by informed voting expresses the irrepressible hope of Christians that in spite of all alarms God is the Lord of history, and that human life is a gift to be claimed from his hand, both here and hereafter.

II. Our second chief concern in this election year is the opposite extremity to apathy. It is the sudden emergence of aggressive religious partisanship in the political arena. We insist that the use of religious radio and TV and local pulpits in support of particular candidates in the name of God distorts Christian truth and threatens American religious freedom.

As Christians we share some important commitments with the so-called Moral Majority: to the home, to the family, to the Bible—though our understanding of reverence for Scripture compels us to resist any narrow or bullying use of biblical texts. But with our brothers and sisters of the popular TV ministry we too cherish God and country. The stars and stripes of our national banner are conspicuous in many Episcopal Churches, and we offer Eucharist on the 4th of July.

As your bishops, we speak out now because the silence of the conventional churches is partly to blame for the impact of this new coalition of strident voices. But we do not form a power lobby—for two reasons.

First, because we are American traditionalists with regard to religion. The founders who fashioned our Constitution of the United States had great respect for the spiritual core of all human experience. But they believed the religious reality, at bottom, is intensely personal. They were also close in time to some events in American colonial history which saw Churches snarling at each other, unable to tolerate a pluralist denominational social order. Therefore, if the individual right to religious belief and practice were to be upheld, Americans had to be protected, not only against an authoritarian anti-religious state (as has emerged in Communism) but also against a tyrannical religious monopoly.

The American colonial period is filled with instances of denominational control of parts of the colonies where deviation from territorial orthodoxy was punishable—and often cruelly.

Puritan Massachusetts banished Quakers from their state on pain of death. In Quaker Pennsylvania during that period all citizens were subject to religious restrictions. An act passed in 1700 required all citizens to attend Church on Sunday or prove they had been at home reading the Scriptures. Failure to do so was subject to fines.

Anglicans in Virginia, at about the same time, pushed through a law which defined orthodoxy for Christians. Denial of Old and New Testament authority was illegal. Offenders could be barred from public office.

Although Maryland was opened initially to Roman Catholics under Lord Baltimore, elsewhere in the colonies life for many of that Church was hindered by the weight of repressive legislation and popular contempt.

When it came time to document religious freedom with Constitutional guarantees, the founders, well versed in history and human behavior, denied the government all power to establish religion. Also denied was the power of the government to interfere with the free exercise of religion. Our founding fathers' argument was never against faith, but against monopoly and political power under religious auspices.

Our refusal in 1980 to entangle religion in partisan politics, and our wariness of contemporary movements that do, is rooted in a wise American tradition of avoiding the almost certain risk of political tyranny in the name of God.

Our second reason for warning against a religious power bloc in the political arena is our certainty that "power" is not the last word in our relationship with God. In the wilderness struggle of Jesus, "power" is the Devil's final word, not God's. Satan's trump temptation is to deliver into Jesus' hands "all the kingdoms of the world and the glory of them" (St. Matthew 4:8).

The response of Jesus to this third seduction defines forever the Christian's relationship to the world: not control, but ministry. Our Lord scorns a ministry founded on any sovereignty but servanthood. Servanthood means the readiness of love to sacrifice and to suffer.

Christ bids us take up the Cross, not a cudgel. We therefore summon ourselves and our people to cheerful service in Christ's love. Be courageous in conviction, tolerant of diversity, and thankful for a political heritage that is ours by gift of human struggle and divine mercy.   Amen.

News Release—October 16, 1980

Chattanooga, Tenn.—The Episcopal Church's House of Bishops has become one of the first mainline church groups to speak out against the formation of religious power blocs that have sprung up this year.

In a strongly-worded statement that was passed by a round of applause, the House declared that "'power' was the Devil's final word, not God's" and that Jesus' response to the temptations in the desert "defines forever the Christian's relationship to the world: not control, but ministry."

The issue of the role of newly-emergent religious political groups was raised the first full day of the Bishops' Oct. 2-9 interim meeting at the Read House here when Bishop Edmond Browning of Hawaii introduced a resolution asking that the pastoral letter deal "at least in part" with that issue. His request was amended to ask the Letter Committee to develop a statement of Christian responsibility in exercising the right to vote.

A pastoral letter becomes a major piece of policy because Canons require that it be read from the pulpit or made available to every parishioner and the bishops paid special attention to the timeliness of this matter by hand-carrying copies away and undertaking the parochial distribution themselves.

Browning's resolution passed the House on Oct. 3, and on Oct. 7, the Pastoral Letter committee chairman, Bishop Bennett Sims of Atlanta, presented draft copies to the bishops who then studied it and suggested changes. The final document was debated during the afternoon of Oct. 8.

From the start of that debate, it was clear that the more than 100 bishops were in general agreement on the thrust of the document and were working to make it as strong a statement as possible.

The 90-minute debate focused on changes in wording to clarify or strengthen the position with only one substantive disagreement. Attempts by Bishops Paul Moore of New York and John Krumm of Europe to rewrite a statement on abortion failed and subsequent efforts to have that portion reconsidered also failed. Moore and Krumm were concerned that the phrase "resist irresponsible and indiscriminate abortion as a heedless, casual birth control option" did not adequately restate a long-held General Convention position but they were unable to convince a majority of their brothers.

After the final approval by applause, an effort to reduce it to a "position paper" in deference to the Church outside the United States was defeated. Such a move would have denied the paper the wide hearing that the bishops sought and Sims was asked instead to include language in the introduction to make it more inclusive.

Concerns Regarding the Moral Majority

Tulsa Council of Churches Statement, Tulsa Oklahoma, September, 1980

The recent Tulsa area appearances by Texas evangelist James Robison and national Moral Majority leader Jerry Falwell have drawn attention to the growing strength of the coalition of religious and political conservatives in the political and public life of our nation.

Generally, the Moral Majority and aligned groups' efforts are aimed at increasing military spending for developing and deploying new nuclear strategic weapons (and building up the armed forces), resuming the peacetime draft, defeating the Equal Rights Amendment, ending school busing for racial desegregation, promoting the teaching of the Genesis theory of creation in the schools, denying civil rights to homosexuals, and working to pass constitutional amendments to prevent abortions and to prescribe prayer in public schools.

While recognizing the right of the Moral Majority to express its aims, such expression opens the issue for public debate and scrutiny. Thus, with questions arising daily concerning the stance and impact of the Moral Majority, a number of concerns are beginning to emerge within portions of the religious community. Tulsa Metropolitan Ministry, as the Tulsa area's interdenominational and interreligious agency, has perceived and assembled these concerns as follows:

A "Christian" agenda: To assert that there is a "Christian" agenda to be imposed on society ignores the fact and value of pluralism: within the Christian community there are different agendas. In other religious and secular communities, there are also different agendas. We feel that the imposition of any one group's agenda on society ignores the fundamental right of the other groups to exist as full members of our national community.

The biblical base: The Moral Majority seems to assume absolute correctness in its interpretation of Scripture, especially as it is applied to issues such as arms control and the rights of minority persons, women and homosexuals. Again, this ignores the plurality of Scriptural interpretation. And, of great concern, absent from the assumptions of the Moral Majority, is Scripture's clear call for justice and mercy, especially for the poor in our midst.

The "electronic" church: "Electronic" ministries have tended to draw resources away from addressing needs of congregations, their members and those in need within their own communities. TMM is committed to maintaining and furthering the vitality of local congregations as the most important manifestation of each religious tradition. The emergence of the Moral Majority through the "electronic" church raises questions for us about how values are formed. In a congregation, people develop values within a community. Where does such give and take occur in a one-way media of persuasion?

The family: We believe that the Moral Majority's stereotype of the family ignores the large number of those who are not in a traditional family lifestyle, and does not adequately take into account the social forces affecting the family. It also seems to us that the family is used by the Moral Majority to de-emphasize or avoid the Scriptural mandates to seek justice and to meet the needs of those who are different from ourselves.

Nationhood and military spending: The Moral Majority has aligned itself with those who define national security in terms of military supremacy and nuclear first-strike capability and with those who define national interest in terms of dominance. First, we question whether or not any nation has the right to claim morality for itself. Second, along with several religious bodies, we question whether or not national security is enhanced by escalation of the arms race. Third, we see that increased military spending can only mean that more people go hungry.

The "Moral Majority": We feel that all persons of faith must discern what is moral. No one group can claim that its historically relative position on morality is God's own definition of morality. Second, we know of no religious tradition which systematically equates morality with the viewpoint of a majority.

TMM's conviction and experience have led to a deep appreciation for the delicate balance between convictions and values and power and the leaders who wield it. America has a rich pluralism, religiously and culturally, which must be nourished if the values of democracy and religious freedom and the dream of providing adequate resources for a "quality of life" for all its citizens are to be realized.

The Quest of "The Christian Position" in the Political Arena

Oklahoma Council of Churches Statement, October, 1980

Many groups and individuals—who represent what is often called evangelical background—have become deeply involved in the political process this year. The Moral Majority, Christian Voice, and Religious Roundtable are but a few of the expressions which seem designed to elect politicians who will be "moral," "religious," or "Christian."

We are members of churches which have sought through the years to shape the climate in which people live and grow, which have been concerned about the whole of life, which have eschewed the fragmentation of spiritual from economic or social realms, and which have paid a price for trying to state unpopular truths before the populace.

As such, we welcome into the political-social-economic arena all who would strive to relate moral and religious convictions to issues in our society. We covet the involvement of evangelicals and all other persons of commitment in the struggle for greater justice and well-being for all persons.

We would raise some words of caution, however. First, we have learned—sometimes with difficulty—to be careful about equating Christian goals with specific candidates. Issues are frequently complex and involve a mixture of good and less-than-good; but persons are always complex and ambiguous. Support of individual candidates is necessary as Christians decide which imperfect persons are most likely to further the goals they seek. Uncritical endorsement which ignores the humanity of candidates is, however, dangerously naive.

Secondly, we warn about the temptation—so often associated with religious conviction—to identify God's ways with ours. Those claiming to be the "Moral Majority" or the "Christian Voice"

Adaptation of material from the National Council of Churches Executive Committee Statement.

appear to offer the only Christian stance regarding societal issues. Religious or moral fervor can quickly lead to claims of exclusive and absolute knowledge about God's will. The results can be powerfully misguided. Further, that stance curtails dialogue with other groups of religious and moral persons and people of good will, a dialogue through which God might reveal His will more clearly.

As citizens, Christians must not abdicate their responsibility because there is no "pure" candidate, no absolutely correct and clear course of action. God's grace frees Christians to "think our way to a sober estimate based on the measure of faith that God has dealt to each of us" (Romans 12:3). Christians may not agree on all political decisions, but they are enjoined not to hold one another in contempt, for all stand before God's tribunal. In the tempering fires of political compromise and accommodations to the needs and interests of many diverse groups, there can be discerned no exclusively "Christian vote;" nor can single issue pressures serve the best interests of our total society. Through a study of scripture, the heritage of churches struggling to be faithful, and through the experiences of life which God opens, Christians are called upon to respond to the demands of the times and the promises of God.

Third, though we believe in the witness and leaven of Christians, we are sensitive to the diversity within our society. To seek to impose "Christian values" on others may ignore their basic right to exist and enter any debate about directions and goals. No one group can define morality for all others. It is a denial of the American tradition to use the power of the state to coerce personal piety or to impose a particular form of religious expression.

In some parts of the world to declare oneself a Christian is to become politically suspect. U.S. Christians can rejoice that this is not true in the United States. The U.S. does not demand political conformity along religious or ideological lines, a heritage of religious and civil liberty to be treasured.

Fourth, we call attention to the fact that within the Christian community varying moral positions are frequently held. To assume that all Christians have an identical perspective on issues like the Equal Rights Amendment, Salt II, defense spending, and sex education is possible only if some decide that dissenters are no longer Christians. That is an assumption we have found unacceptable. Only those who are convinced that their own interpretation of Scripture is absolutely correct can be so exclusive. Many of us are convinced that the stance publicly taken by the "Moral Majority," for example, is unbalanced, and not in accord with all of the Biblical mandates of morality and justice and compassion.

Fifth, we are troubled by the tactics of some which directly or indirectly judge persons to be immoral or unchristian because they reach a different position on complex issues. Such judgments about the character and motives of others is in danger of being unjust, simplistic, and self-righteous.

Christians have obligations of citizenship to fulfill, particularly the right and duty to vote, as well as the Biblical injunction to work toward a social vision of compassion, justice and peace. God intends for Christians to pursue the "things that make for peace and build up the common life," which would include participation in the political process.

While we are reluctant to criticize another group of Christians who are striving to be faithful, we would respectfully point out to them and to the populace at large that not all Christians are represented by such groups as the so-called Moral Majority or Christian Voice. We perceive excesses and lapses in their positions, and we are aware of a potentially dangerous and uncritical identification of a group of Christians with a particular political ideology.

On Religion and Politics,
by S. Collins Kilburn

The Church Council Bulletin of North Carolina, Fourth Quarter, 1980

In a recent *New York Times* column, Anthony Lewis commented, "If you take a longer view than tomorrow's polls, the most important issue in the 1980 election is not inflation or public policy or unemployment. It is the role of religion in American politics."

Mr. Lewis exaggerates, I believe, but nevertheless the resurgence of an aggressive, politicized fundamentalism has given the issue considerable urgency. Radical right religionists have moved into the political arena in a way that commands attention. This could be an opportunity for all of us because it forces us to think through our own understanding of religion and politics, and it challenges us to get our own act together. Most of us in the mainline, ecumenical churches object to the style, and to much of the content, of the fundamentalist crusading. But, what do we advocate as an alternative: A religion isolated from the public sphere? A religion so far above the mundane political scramble that the two never touch?

We need to be quite clear that we agree with the Falwells of the world on the right and duty of Christians and church bodies to bring moral concerns into the political arena. Several months ago I appeared on a television talk program called "Pro and Con" opposite the Reverend Daniel Carr, the director of Churches for Life and Liberty, a kind of local version of the Moral Majority. Father Joseph Vetter, the editor of the Roman Catholic newspaper in the State, was on the show, too. The moderator threw out the question, "Should churches get involved in politics?" He was frustrated because he could not stir up any disagreement. There were differences between Mr. Carr and myself on tactics and style, but not on the question of involvement. Indeed, Christians ought to be actively engaged in politics, and their political views ought to be informed by the Bible. And church organizations have a responsibility to make their views known on public policy issues.

Some of our friends, repelled by TV crusaders, object in the name of principle of "separation of church and state." That particular phrase is not accurate or helpful in describing what has been or should be the relation between religion and the government of this country. In fact, it is positively misleading. As historian Sidney Mead points out in "The Nation with the Soul of the Church" we have neither a "church" nor a "state" in the traditional sense in this nation. The phrase, "a wall of separation between church and state," used by Thomas Jefferson, is not a part of the U.S. Constitution. Mead recommends John Madison's words—"a line of separation between the rights of religion and of the Civil authority"—as being more precisely descriptive of the American way. A wall is a solid, unchanging, impenetrable structure. A "line" is a moving point, which might zigzag in places. It is a fluid image.

The constitution and the First Amendment laid down as guidelines very general, abstract principles in terms of no religious test for national office, no "establishment of religion," and no prohibition of the "free exercise thereof." What these principles would mean in practice no one could anticipate. That was left to be determined as specific questions arose. In any case, they cannot mean that religious groups are prohibited from attempting to influence government.

So, we agree with the fundamentalists on this point. There is a sharp difference, however, in the understanding of the relation of the Divine will to particular measures. In my debate with Mr. Carr, I stated that no particular piece of legislation, no specific public policy, could be said to represent the absolute will of God; and, further that, no human being can say that he/she knows with utter certainty that a specific provision is in line with God's intentions. In other words, one should never speak of THE Christian or THE Biblical position on a public question. I may feel very strongly, and believe with a high degree of certainty, that, for example, Christians should support food assistance for the hungry or the Equal Rights Amendment. But I should never claim to know the mind of God with absolute confidence on such questions. Nor should I claim that there is absolutely clear endorsement for such measures in the Bible. We cannot move in a straight line from the Bible to a particular policy. The Bible informs our minds, shapes our values and opens our eyes to see human need. But it does not tell us how to vote on House Bill 523.

The fundamentalists seem to have few similar reservations. They imply that there is an unambiguous Biblical position on a whole string of things from the Panama Canal Treaty to a legislative measure encouraging coordination between agencies serving children (New Generation Act). Some of these claims are so farfetched that they diminish the credibility of those who make them. More serious than that, however, is that this way of theologizing breeds fanaticism and self-righteousness. All of us have to guard against this sin and keep in mind the truth of Reinhold

Niebuhr's observation: "The sad experiences of Christian history show how human pride and spiritual arrogance rise to new heights precisely at the point where the claims of sanctity are made without due qualifications."

Most readers of this *Bulletin* would agree pretty readily, I surmise, with these words of caution about identifying the gospel too closely with any political program. So now let me suggest that the main problem for us in the mainline churches is generally in the opposite direction. And while we criticize the fundamentalists for their aggressive fanaticism, we need to criticize ourselves even more vigorously for our timidity and our lack of any kind of zeal for advocacy in the public arena. Richard Neuhaus in one of his books *(Christian Faith and Public Policy)* cautions against "ringing manifestos" and "prophetic pronouncements" which are sometimes merely the posturing of unwarranted certitude. He goes on to say, however, that "the greater and more common sin of Christians, is to be paralyzed by uncertainty. It is a failure of courage and, finally, a failure of faith; it is the refusal to live and act, also in the political realm, in radical obedience upon God's forgiving and correcting love."

There is some overlap, but by and large the ecumenical churches have a different set of moral concerns to bring to the political forum: international cooperation and a reversal of the nuclear arms race; the alleviation of poverty and the empowerment of the powerless at home and around the world; careful stewardship of natural resources; and the elimination of inequality based on race and sex. These concerns require political implementation. We know, as well as we can know anything, that they represent, in general terms, God's intentions for the human family. Can we not learn to pursue these goals with zeal, fervor and effectiveness without becoming high-handed or fanatical; without identifying the gospel too closely with a particular political program or party, and without getting into the business of endorsing candidates or labeling candidates "Christian" or "unChristian"? Can we not learn to enter the political fray, on fire for justice, but as servants, and not as a religious power bloc? This, I believe, is the challenge which the politicized fundamentalism presents to us.

A Resolution

Adopted by the Presbyterian Church U.S. Synod of the Mid-South, September 9, 1980

Whereas, there have arisen recently activist organizations that are supporting and opposing candidates for public office on the claimed basis of the candidates' Christian belief and moral stance, and,

Whereas, the religious and moral integrity of many public officials is being questioned and ridiculed on the basis of their position on a few political issues, and,

Whereas, ministers and churches within the Synod of the Mid-South are being circularized by these groups, are being encouraged to join in with their political activities and are being instructed in how to support candidates and programs without losing the church's tax exempt status, and,

Whereas, our belief in the perfect holiness and the complete sovereignty of God, as expressed in the first and second commandments, and our confession of the reality and pervasiveness of human sinfulness prevents us from identifying any human leader, any group, any government, any political system or any party platform with the will of God or as the work of God, and,

Whereas, the right and responsibility of the church to exercise its prophetic role by addressing issues arising in the political arena, and the right and responsibility of individual church members to endorse and support specific candidates and political programs must be defended and affirmed, nevertheless the Presbyterian Church, U.S. has never considered it proper for churches to endorse specific political candidates or platforms:

Therefore be it resolved:

1. That the Synod of the Mid-South of the Presbyterian Church in the U.S. express its dismay at the arrogance of these groups which would presume to discredit the Christian conviction and commitment of public officials because of a difference in political viewpoint.
2. That the Synod of the Mid-South re-affirm its support of the separation of church and state and strongly voice its disapproval of any church or church-related group which, either overtly or covertly, endorses or supports candidates for political office, and,
3. That the Synod of the Mid-South, through its constituent presbyteries, call all ministers and sessions to guard against being used by such groups or becoming involved in their activities.

McCoy Franklin
Commissioner from
John Knox Presbytery

Resolution adopted by the Presbyterian Church U.S. Presbytery of Mecklenburg, September 23, 1980.

Whereas, the United States is in an election year when voters' choices will have profound impact upon state and national policies, priorities and programs, and

Whereas, organizations, such as Moral Majority, Inc., Churches for Life and Liberty (in North Carolina), Carolinians for Biblical Morality (in South Carolina), are demonstrating significant influence upon the outcome of elections in various parts of the country, be it

Resolved, that the Presbytery of Mecklenburg, meeting on September 23, 1980, affirm:

1. That while it is appropriate for Christians to form organizations for political action, it is pretentious for any organization or individual to claim to have "the" Christian, or "the" moral, or "the" Biblical position on any given issue; and

2. That it is deplorable when any organization in zeal for its cause resorts to half-truths and intolerance; and
3. That it is important for citizens not to be intimidated by the religious and political rhetoric of an organization but to take seriously the injunction of I John 4:1 to "test the spirits to see whether they are of God; for many false prophets have gone out into the world;" and be it

Resolved further, That the Stated Clerk send a copy of this resolution to all ministers and Clerks of Session of Mecklenburg Presbytery and to the editors of *The Presbyterian Survey, The Presbyterian News, The Presbyterian Outlook,* and *The Presbyterian Journal.*

Bill Moyers Journal

Campaign Report #3 (Excerpt from television transcript) WNET/THIRTEEN

I know the people in this report. I was born and reared among them; they're my kin. Although long ago I made passage to another place and culture, to another way of seeing and believing, I still hear at certain times with affection echoes of their prayers and hymns. I recognize deeply imprinted within me the inherited yearning for order and authority that caused them in menacing times to cleave more tenaciously to their faith. It isn't surprising that they're fighting back against the discoveries of science, decrees of government, and dilemmas of democracy that intrude upon their fixed scheme of things. Nor is it unprecedented for people of a religious persuasion to want to affect the system, to matter politically, to try to elect to office agents of their anger who will attempt to supply the leadership for which they ache. There are precedents aplenty. I once wrote a speech for Lyndon Johnson asking Southern Baptists to rally behind the Voting Rights Act of 1965. A Catholic bishop urges his parishioners to vote for candidates who oppose abortion. Jimmy Carter prowls black churches as if they were precincts of the Democratic Party, which many are. William Sloane Coffin marshals his congregation to march on the Pentagon, and Jews pressure Washington to support Israeli government decisions based on interpretations of scriptures from the Bronze Age, precedents all. It is not that the evangelicals are taking politics seriously that bothers me. It's the lie they're being told by the demagogues who flatter them into believing they can achieve politically the certitude they have embraced theologically. The world doesn't work that way. There is no heaven on earth. Nor can our democracy agree to a moral majority that makes religious doctrine the test of political opinion. You may have that only where all are alike in thought and root and intent, which America is not. Here, the idea has long been to protect religious freedom from a carnivorous state, political deliberation from dogmatic zealots, and militant believers from one another. So they're being misled, these people, by manipulators of politics masquerading as messengers of heaven, and their hearts will be broken by false gods who, having taken the coin of their vote or purse, will move on to work the next crowd. The same Reverend Falwell who claims a divine mandate to go right into the halls of Congress and fight for laws that will save America is caught lying in public about a meeting he had with the president. Ronald Reagan, having endorsed the moral majority in Dallas, moves on to a luncheon given for him by teamsters in Ohio whose chieftains include four men either indicted or convicted or being investigated for corrupt practices. Some majority. Some morality.

Right-Wing Extremism

Union of American Hebrew Congregations Resolution, San Francisco, California, November 22, 1980

We applaud the president of the Union for alerting us to important issues which are of great concern to us at this time.

The rise of extremism in some elements of American life—including episodes of anti-Semitism and the growing impact of the

Radical Right—represents a clear and present danger to the tradition of American pluralism and a distortion of religious precepts in political life. The Reform Jewish movement has always had a commitment to the ethical values of Judaism and their relevance to contemporary society. This prophetic mandate assumes new urgency today because of the rise of extremism, both theological and political.

We see these developments as a threat to the fabric of American life, to a democratic society, to Jewish values and to the security of American Jewry. The great strength of America lies in its pluralistic nature with its respect for diversity of viewpoints, whether liberal or conservative, Christian, Jewish or any other.

Therefore, the Board of Trustees of the Union of American Hebrew Congregations resolves:

1. To give high priority to a program of religious action to strengthen human rights and human dignity, thus serving not only a prophetic mission, but equally our own interests, for we Jews have a profound stake in maintaining an open, tolerant and compassionate society.
2. To reach out to religious (Jewish and non-Jewish), civic and minority groups to form coalitions which will advance our mutual concerns.
3. To urge our congregations to advance these goals through the strengthening of existing religious action committees or establishing such vital entities where none exist. We encourage all congregations to take advantage of the resources of our Washington Religious Action Center and urge individual congregants to keep informed of developing issues by subscribing to the CHAI/IMPACT information system.
4. To establish a joint task force of the Commission on Social Action and the Commission on Synagogue Administration which will provide guidance and assistance to those congregations which experience incidents of violence and vandalism, and to provide guidance on preventive measures to all of our congregations.

Statement by Religious Leaders to President Ford and Governor Carter, October 18, 1976

As representatives from the Evangelical, Protestant, Roman Catholic and Jewish communities in the United States, we call upon President Ford and Governor Carter to repudiate appeals to religious bigotry in the current election campaign.

When, during the Presidential primaries, prejudice appeared about to surface against the Evangelical community, responsible spokesmen warned against any appeals to sectarian bigotry toward this large segment of the American people.

Religious bigotry has in fact remained gratifyingly absent from the Presidential race, but it has become alarmingly evident in a number of Congressional contests. Reportedly, drives have been mounted in at least 30 districts to elect "God-centered citizens" who will work to "rebuild" America as a "Christian republic." Such efforts have involved both Democrats and Republicans.

For example, in a Republican Senatorial primary in Arizona, a Jewish candidate received anti-Semitic calls and threats, and his opponent is reported to have told Evangelical audiences: "We need to elect a Christian Congress."

In a five-sided Democratic Congressional primary in Texas, candidates were questioned in detail about their religious beliefs, and their replies were publicly "rated."

At other levels of political and civic life, too, attempts have recently been made to impose a religious test, which violates the U.S. Constitution. In one case in North Carolina, school board candidates were questioned about their religious convictions for the "information" of voters.

The campaigns are led by a loose coalition of organizations with common goals and interlocking directorates which issue literature, send out regional representatives to screen and influence political candidates, or seek to mobilize grass-roots support for a political movement of and for "real Christians only."

The announced purpose of the drives is to raise "the moral quality" of American politics—a goal which Americans of all faiths and persuasions can share. But Americans cannot share the underlying assumptions: that candidates for office are to be judged on grounds other than their political and civic qualifications—and that non-Christian believers, nonbelievers, or even Christians with a different religious commitment are less qualified, trustworthy or patriotic.

These assumptions strike at the heart of the American democratic process and, even more fundamentally, at the principle of separation between church and state.

Religious freedom, based on the separation principle, has been the keystone of all our other freedoms—and ever since Colonial times, Evangelical Baptists, Methodists and other non-establishment religious groups have been second to no one in making it so. Freedom of religion has also made possible our pluralistic society, with its capacity for negotiating and reconciling religious conflicts and differences that have so often plunged other societies into strife, misery and bloodshed.

To create religious voting blocs on the American scene would be to discard these historic achievements—to invite a return of religious strife or oppression. It could bring us back to the conditions of Colonial times, when theocratic rulers withheld religious liberty from the people.

‘We urge the Presidential candidates as leaders of their respective parties, as well as the parties' National State and Local Committees, to reject forcefully any campaign appeals based on the religion a candidate may profess.

Episcopalian Bishop Paul Moore; Fr. Joseph O'Hare, Editor-in-Chief of *America;* Dr. Arnold L. Olson, Evangelical Free Church of America and former president of the National Association of Evangelicals; and Rabbi Marc H. Tanenbaum, National Director, Interreligious Affairs, of the American Jewish Committee.

Polemical Uses of Religion in Current Political Controversies

Union Theological Faculty Statement, September 25, 1980

Twenty-five members of the faculty of Union Theological Seminary in their regular monthly meeting on Wednesday, September 24, passed the following resolution regarding recent "polemical uses of religion in current political controversies."

Union Theological Seminary, founded in 1836, is a non-denominational graduate school of religion located in New York City. Dr. Donald W. Shriver, Jr. is President of the Faculty and.William E. Dodge Professor of Applied Christianity.

The resolution reads as follows:

"We speak as a Christian theological faculty with a shared concern for the relation of our faith to our citizenship. Disturbed by some of the polemical uses of religion in current political controversies, we make these affirmations:

1. We believe that the God of justice and love responds to the prayers of people of diverse religious traditions. We deplore denial of the inherent dignity of all God's human creation. As Christians we are offended by the recent assertion of a church leader that "God Almighty does not hear the prayer of a Jew." We, who often use the prayer of the Jewish Jesus of Nazareth, believe that God hears and values the prayers of Jews as truly as those of Christians.

2. We believe that all persons and religious communities have a responsibility to discover and act upon the meaning of their faith for political life. On the other hand we believe that no church or religious group has an exclusive claim upon Scripture interpretation, ethical insight, or political wisdom. There is in the Christian gospel no ground for "boasting" (Romans 3:27). In the civil covenant of our society, we expect our own insights as well as those of others to be enlarged and corrected as all appreciate the experiences of the variety of people who make up this nation and world."

Signed by the following members of the Faculty of Union Theological Seminary:

Richard D. Spoor	Ardith S. Hayes	Sidney Skirvin
Malcolm L. Warford	T. Richard Snyder	Robert T. Handy
Geoffrey Wainwright	James A. Martin, Jr.	Roger L. Shinn
Kosuke Koyama	Thomas L. Robinson	Milton McC. Gatch
William B. Kennedy	Mary D. Pellauer	Janet R. Walton
George M. Landes	James A. Forbes, Jr.	Donald W. Shriver, Jr.
Robert E. Neale	Richard A. Norris, Jr.	Beverly W. Harrison
James M. Washington	Gerald T. Sheppard	Robert Seaver
Tom F. Driver		

Church vs. Politics:
The Moment of Truth

Editorial, *The Orthodox Church,* **November, 1980**

Times are changing. Throughout the turbulent sixties and seventies—years of revolutionary optimism—a great number of Christians, and particularly the liberal Protestant Establishment which dominated ecumenical agencies, were actively engaged in supporting political causes, proclaiming that Christians have no right to remain indifferent to injustice, racism, discrimination and other forms of social oppression. Political conservatives were then supporting Christian non-involvement in politics.

In the past two or three years, however, the scene has changed. Not only the "Right to Life Movement," which encourages political struggle against legislation permitting abortion, but Protestant conservatives, who tend to maintain the traditional Protestant identification of Christianity with the virtues of capitalism, are actively engaged in open political activity in order to find legal support for their views and beliefs.

It is time, therefore, that both sides transcend the hypocritical self-righteousness with which they accuse their opponents of "mixing religion with politics." In fact—and especially in a democratic society—an "apolitical" stance is impossible. Even abstention from voting invites a condonement of the status quo, which is itself a political attitude. On the other hand, the Christian faith, which announces the coming of an eternal Kingdom of God, also implies that the disciples of Jesus are sent into the world in order to transform and transfigure it.

The real danger for Christians lies not in political activity as such, but in a loss of their Christian identity. In fighting the horrors of racism, discrimination and oppression, the liberals of the sixties were (and still are) often unaware of the danger of jumping on the bandwagon of secular revolutionary ideologies whose ultimate goal is not to protect human dignity, but to destroy it. In struggling against abortion legislation, which amounts to an even more horrible and self-righteous legal genocide of innocent human beings, the conservative Christians of today should equally be aware that their activity will lose its integrity if it is pursued in an unholy alliance with a reawakened Ku Klux Klan, or simply and naively integrated into the ideology of a "business as usual" capitalist society.

In a democratic society, politics are unavoidable, but they are generally divisive and dirty. The Christian faith and the values it implies will simply cease to be credible if it is reduced to political games and identified with electoral ambitions. Individually, Christians cannot always stay above politics, but the defense of Christian values should.

—FR. JOHN MEYENDORFF

Politics as Matrix for Religion

Editorial, *National Catholic Reporter,* **September 26, 1980**

While Pope John Paul II tries to pull priests out of politics, Protestant TV preachers and other ministers are jumping in. And they're jumping to the right. They unabashedly use their money, their influence and often their pulpits to promote positions remarkably similar to items in the Republican platform—items put there by the most conservative GOP leaders.

(Were an equal number of influential Catholic clergy—assuming we had them—so blatantly political, there would be an uproar, and latent anti-Catholic bigotry would quickly surface.)

Not all Protestants by any means are turning right with the Republicans. A recent Gallup poll shows that most evangelical Protestants support President Carter. But the publicity and momentum belong to the religious right that is pushing positions and candidates it calls pro-family/anti-ERA, anti-communist, anti-big government, anti-secular humanist.

Many Catholics also support these positions and candidates. Catholics especially have been leaders in that part of the pro-family political movement that is pro-life/anti-abortion. The most recent Catholic effort was the recent vain attempt by Boston's Cardinal Humberto Medeiros to influence the Massachusetts primary. In a pastoral letter, he said, "Those who make abortions possible by law—such as legislators and those who promote, defend and elect the same lawmakers—cannot separate themselves totally from that guilt which accompanies this horrendous crime and deadly sin. If you are for true human freedom—and for life—you will follow your conscience when you vote, you will vote to save 'our children, born and unborn.' "

Medeiros, certainly no right-winger, did not influence voters enough to defeat the two Democratic congressional candidates who advocate free choice abortions and government money for poor women's abortions.

There are several points to make about mixing religion and politics. First, we are for it. Politics is the way people's values can influence U.S. social mores. Many of our most cherished American values have a basis in religion, particularly the Judeo-Christian tradition. While the separation of official churches from the state is a great asset to our society, there is no possible way to separate people's religious values from politics. Church-state separation and religion-politics are different things. One is desirable, the other is impossible.

One person's religious value is sometimes another person's social evil. Which brings us to the second point. It looks as if many people who cherish conservative/evangelical religion have been seduced or coopted by right-wing politicians. For example, it's difficult to see how people who are pro-life, against killing the unborn, could also advocate the death penalty, more nuclear weapons and a belligerent military/foreign policy that is likely to get us into the horrible killings of warfare. And it is difficult, for example, to see how the Christian gospel, which professes works of mercy, compassion and help for the poor, squares with regressive taxes and slashed welfare budgets that punish the poor. Yet the right-wing religious/political leaders are connecting these contradictory positions.

Third, the great contribution to the mix of religion and politics that Catholics could make is not being made. It is sound traditional Catholic teaching to emphasize social responsibility for our children, and for all people, the "born and unborn." The body of Catholic social justice teaching, proclaimed dramatically by John Paul II, is unexcelled.

Although one might argue with some positions regarding human sexuality (and abortion is *not* in that category) of the U.S. bishops, their official positions on social and economic political issues are generally humane. Catholic voters and politicians should not hesitate to advocate and work hard for these vital religious values in politics.

It is also sound, traditional Catholic teaching to urge voters to follow their consciences, as Medeiros did, but it can be extremely difficult to decide how to vote. Some on the right wing have developed a "Christian hit list" of liberal legislators. Usually the targeted politicians have two things in common: they are not against abortion and they are for "liberal" legislation that helps the poor, limits military spending and regulates big business. They are not pro-life for the unborn, but they are certainly pro-life for the born.

Let us suppose that the opposing candidates are against abortion but also against other "liberal," pro-life legislation for the born. It becomes difficult for a conscientious voter to choose wisely. Then the mix of religion and politics gets down to some of the terrible challenges that are the responsibility of every voter. It's time Catholics did a better job of mixing in their religious values.

A Moral America

Campaign Issues—5, Editorial, *The Christian Science Monitor*,
October 27, 1980

Seldom in recent history has the question of morality come so
strongly to the fore. The moral and spiritual fiber of the United
States is being severely tested on matters as private as abortion,
sexual conduct, and family life—and as public as justice for blacks,
women, minorities; compassion for the world's poor; noninter-
ference in the internal affairs of other nations; and the fostering of
human rights for peoples everywhere. It is widely recognized that
America must have a strong moral and spiritual foundation.
Without such a foundation, society grows lawless and stagnant; it
loses its compass.

But morality must be built within the thoughts and lives of
individuals and then translated into the nation's laws and policies
through the democratic process. It cannot be imposed by the state
either on individuals or on nations. And it is not Christian morality
that lapses into bigotry, self-righteousness, or pious preachiness.

This election year finds Americans pondering these issues
because of the emergence of religion as a political force.
Significantly, perhaps, it is not only the Islamic world that is
witnessing a resurgence of religious fundamentalism, with the
difficulties this poses for democratic government. In the U.S., too,
we see the merging of the Christian "new right" with the political
right into a theocratic force that seeks to dominate the political
process. The trend is worrisome.

Let us say at the outset that we understand the reasons for the
religious revival. Many Americans feel deeply the need for a
national moral awakening, for a turning back from what is seen to
be a more and more permissive society. The fears are not
unfounded. No one of the Judeo-Christian faith can fail to be
concerned about the widespread immorality, the rise in out-of-

wedlock births, the increased use of hard drugs by the young, the growth of pornography, the indecency portrayed in novels, on television, and even flaunted in the news magazines. America indeed needs to be shaken out of its unthinking tolerance of these trends. To the extent that Christian fundamentalists bring these issues to public notice, their efforts have value. An aroused public is a necessary prelude to constructive reform.

It is the method of correction which must be watched, however. All too often religious activism is narrowly and simplistically bound up with one issue, such as abortion or the Equal Rights Amendment. Some Christian groups go so far as to use "moral scorecards" to rate the performance of public figures on such unrelated issues as school prayer, the defense treaty with Taiwan, and the formation of a Department of Education. When self-appointed groups set out to decide who is moral and what a "Christian position" is, they risk practicing moral zealotry and destroying good public servants. The results can be incongruous, and often hardly moral in themselves. Such an able senator as John Glenn, for instance, who is an elder in the Presbyterian church, is rated zero by one ultra-conservative organization. Congressman Richard Kelly, implicated in the Abscam bribery investigation, merits 100.

What is needed for righteous government is not to elect those who supposedly hold the right view on a single or even several issues. It is, in the words of an editorial in *Christianity Today,* "to secure responsible political leaders of intelligence, deep moral commitment, political wisdom and administrative skills." Leaders, in other words, of probity who have the ability to govern.

It must be remembered that America is an increasingly pluralistic society, an amalgam of different races, cultures, nationalities, religions. Even the dominant Judeo-Christian religious groups differ as to their interpretation of biblical teaching and the practice of Christianity. In these conditions Americans can only be grateful for the Constitution's wisdom of erecting a wall of separation between church and state and leaving religious practice to individual conscience. For one group to insist on formal public prayer in school, for instance, smacks of dictating religion to those who may pray differently or not at all. Similarly, to provide tax aid for religious schools, as Ronald Reagan advocates, would put the government in the business of supporting religion. Surely religious tolerance is best safeguarded when the state injects itself the least.

This is not to say that government has to be morally neutral or that Christian religious groups should play no part in the political process. Few would argue that church groups should go so far as to tell citizens how to vote. But they have every right to speak out on social and political issues if they wish, to participate in national debate, to point to unethical behavior in or out of government. Christians of all denominations in fact need to weigh in more in the democratic process if laws, court decisions, and public policies are to reflect the highest standards of morality. Religious tolerance must not mean tolerance of drugs, pornography, antifamily laws—all of which cry out for public indictment. It is simply the single-issue moral absolutism and parochialism we deplore.

A moral America encompasses more than an obligation to protect human life—and abortion is a practice we oppose but which involves such complex issues as to be best left to individual conscience and choice. Morality involves the whole tone of society—the integrity of government leaders, the ethics of corporate business, and the sensitivity of schools, universities, news media, and the arts and entertainment industry to purifying the nation's cultural as well as physical environment. It means addressing such problems as justice for blacks and other minorities, equal rights for women (recognized even by many opponents of ERA), and training of the unemployed. Is it morally tolerable that millions of people cannot find work, that joblessness among black youth, in particular, runs a high 40 percent?

Looking abroad, few would deny that America should stand for principle in the conduct of its affairs. Toward this end, reform efforts must continue to assure that U.S. policy remains free of such undemocratic practices of the past as interfering in other countries' electoral processes.

President Carter's early focus on human rights did much to lend a moral dimension to foreign policy, but in execution the policy often left the U.S. seeming merely moralistic and naive. We would have the U.S. continue to hold high the banner of universal human rights and to use every prudent means to promote them. To neglect this matter would be to abandon the country's traditional ideals—and the very things on which millions of people around the world look to the U.S. for example and leadership.

But there must be the maturity to know that it is a nation's practice rather than its words which ultimately carry weight. For example, can Americans accept that, at a time when there is a rising world demand and competition for energy and other resources, they are often wasteful and inefficient in their own consumption of these resources? Surely out of a sense of justice and of compassion for the less fortunate they can do more to foster economic growth in the third world, and to help husband the earth's bounty in a way that embraces and blesses all.

In the end, too, America's influence for good will depends on what kind of society it is and what it chooses to present to the world as worthy of emulation. In terms of its freedoms, its opportunities, its creativity and innovation, it is still the most revolutionary land on the globe. Yet the U.S. image abroad is at times undercut by practices which tend to obscure positive American contributions. This happens, for instance, when some Americans overseas show off the worst aspects of their culture—tawdry movies and magazines, vulgar music, a materialistic way of life—or when some U.S. business firms export foods, chemicals, and other products which are declared unsafe for domestic use. Those representing the U.S. should respect the cultural and physical environment of other nations as well as their religious and other traditions.

This is not to fail to appreciate the enormous cultural, economic, and political benefits which America has shared and continues to share with those willing to accept them—but merely to point to the need for cultivating moral and spiritual sensitivity in an age of growing global interdependence. The great underlying test of a nation's integrity, after all, lies not only in the virtues of its society but in its demonstrated love for mankind, in doing unto others as it would have others do unto it. This is the ideal for which the people—and their leaders—must unceasingly strive.

Not all Evangelicals Agree on Christianizing America

Editorial by Senator Mark Hatfield

As we approach the 1980 election, new political forces are mixing religion and politics in an unsophisticated and, many are saying, dangerous way.

There is not so much a malaise as a confused spirit coming from disconnected people without emotional and spiritual strength to withstand the demands of a fragmenting and frightening culture. A recent Gallup Poll found that Americans are concerned more about diminished "family life, health and peace of mind," rather than material concerns. But certain religious groups are proclaiming "The country is going to hell . . . and the Christian responsibility is to save it by electing Christians and legislating morality."

Canadian college professor Robert Alan Cook points out there are certain essential characteristics that a democratic society must have to keep it from degenerating as did the ill-fated Weimar republic in post-World War I Germany.

First, there must be resistance to atomization, which reduces to a mass movement frightened and isolated people who no longer identify with traditional values. Fearful and isolated souls flocked to the Nazi banner, and even industrialists and bankers contributed great sums to Hitler because they saw him as a cohesive force in an otherwise impotent world. A breakdown of pluralism and individual values has led to mass movements with quick and simplistic solutions.

Secondly, if a society is to remain strong, it must resist the apathy that was the undoing of the German Weimar Republic in which the far right and far left were making counter charges about its legitimacy, while the vast middle class stood apathetic and apologetic. A growing near majority in America today ignores elections.

Thirdly, a strong democratic society must satisfy people's hunger for wholeness. Tormented souls are not finding peace in astrology,

This editorial originally appeared in *Oregon Statesman-Journal* and was reprinted in *Congressional Record*, October 1, 1980.

the occult, Eastern religion or the simplistic notions of certain new right religionists, who are creating an anti-biblical theology of power politics. For our democracy to remain strong we must participate together in reformulating an effectual national framework to prevent us from becoming hopelessly polarized.

As we critique the religious right's attempt to "Christianize America," it is essential to recall that the movement includes many sincere and concerned people, who have as much right to organize as any other group, and is not the first group to embrace single-issue politics. Further, many critics of the Moral Majority and Christian Voice single-issue politics were, in fact, pioneers of it and are crying alarm about violations of principles of separation of church and state when they themselves have been roundly criticized in the past. And, finally, not all evangelical Protestants and Catholics are in the same camp. The movement is not monolithic. Evangelicalism today is diverse politically.

In fact, many evangelicals share my concern that the grievous sins of our society are militarism and materialism, rather than the Taiwan Treaty or Equal Rights Amendment or the Panama Canal. Also, because the personalities of the leaders are central, ego battles are certain, and new litmus tests based on morality will pass as they fragment the faithful.

We must however, be very pointed that any movement that substitutes a false gospel has to be called to account. There has been some maturing already among leaders of the far right in not persisting in calling people's religious commitments into question because of differences on political issues. But the negative effect on millions of people across the country is measured by mail we receive.

Many pastors and parishioners demand that politicians affirm a certain conservative political ideology. "What think ye of Christ?" is the classic question that provides the only test for Christians. The Apostle Paul states in Colossians 1:26 that "the secret is simply this: Christ in you bringing with Him the hope of all the glorious things to come."

Christian people differ on political issues, and it is legitimate to take opposing positions, just as Sen. Sam Nunn (Democrat from Georgia) and I do on military questions. But a movement that assesses one's salvation on any basis other than the biblical one is apostasy.

It is questionable, and possibly reprehensible, to baptize issues with religious right ideology. To defeat Caesar by becoming Caesar is what Jesus rejected when He wept over Jerusalem in Luke 19 and said, "Would that today you knew the things that make for peace. But now they are hid from your eyes." Jesus refused to become a Caesar. Instead, He laid His life down for His friends as spiritual savior.

The need today is for more sacrificing followers like Mother Teresa of India, who are willing to lay down their lives rather than be power brokers in ecclesiastical trappings. We must guard against zealots who would diminish our freedoms for the sake of their definition of morality. The world has seen that in Iran.

Another danger is idealization of American history by the religious right. Many Christian conservatives have, I think, unwittingly exaggerated the role of religion in American history, making America God's nation of the New Covenant. An organization called Citizens for God and Country, and preachers influenced by it, claim exclusivity for Christian religion and purport that all others are "against the law." It is good to remind ourselves that many of our founding fathers were Deists, children of the Enlightenment, not the Reformation.

Some plead for us to return to our Christian roots with prayer in schools and other specific legislation. This becomes dangerous when idealized history becomes spiritual justification for blind patriotism. An arrogant intolerance is possibly the most frightful side of this "Christianizing America" movement. Practitioners quote the proverb, "When the righteous rule, the people rejoice; when the unrighteous rule, the people mourn." I sense that we should add for a caution that when the self-righteous rule, people are oppressed.

But no matter what the valid criticism, we cannot and must not totally dismiss or scorn the Christian wing of the New Right. The movement is significant on at least three levels. Politically, its potential is to be one of the most powerful forces in America and could well decide who will become or remain president. It will be a significant factor with financial backing and voter registration (it is estimated that there are 12 million potential uninvolved conservative voters).

Spiritually what is at stake is the credibility of the Christian church and the identity of Christianity in a modern, complex world.

And socially profound questions are raised for American and Western society. The movement is a symptom of a deep sense of disenchantment. It gives reason to pause over the similarities of other troublesome times, as in Germany. It raises questions about the moral and spiritual basis of the social order that cannot survive without some legitimation.

We have today little cohesive moral philosophy in our social order. As Meg Greenfield wrote recently, "Government-grown values are by definition and necessity spiritually deformed. They tend to be lowest common denominator generalities or pressure-group-cooked outrages. But we have become so tolerant that we have refused to view practically any indecency, outrage or pathological assault on our sense of rightness as any way but a civil liberties problem."

And if there is no relative consensus about what constitutes meaning then it must be asked if anything other than a dictatorship can result. De Toqueville observed that: "deposition may govern without faith, but liberty cannot." We cannot remove religion from society without grave consequences, but neither can we embrace an idolatry that reduces religion merely to the glue of society.

We of the orthodox Christian faith who are highly committed to having it impact both our corporate life and personal life are impaled, it appears, on the horns of a dilemma . . . the idiocy of saying faith has no impact or the idolatry of embracing state religion. There is no doubt in my mind that the present rise of the Christian right is pushing us toward a resolution of this dilemma or at least toward a desire to live lovingly and at peace in the ambiguity of our "answers" and "solutions."

From my vantage point it seems that there are three broad scenarios possible.

Increased crisis and decline with the present process continuing until democratic society cannot exist; or,

A halt to the crisis through an imposition of traditional values by authoritarian means; or,

National and, in fact worldwide revitalization by a spiritual renewal, similar to that in the 1630s in England or after the Civil War in America.

If the alternatives are as I described, then our situation serves to underline that it is no longer an exaggeration to say that spiritual revival is the key to physical survival, and nothing is more dangerous than false religion, but nothing is as necessary as true religion.

Excerpt from "Let's Get Serious"

Speech by Frank Madison Reid, September, 1980, African Methodist Episcopal Church, Partners in Ecumenism Conference

If we are really serious it means that first of all we must understand that the traditionally mainstream denominations have a fight on their hands that demands that we unite to face the crisis of survival in our times. There are those who would call the new phenomenon an evangelical revolution; others would call it the new reformation. There is a lot about the movement's inflexibility, intolerance and passion for annihilation that makes me think of the Great Inquisition and the Dark Ages. It is estimated that this evangelistic strain of Christianity has in excess of 45 million adherents. Rifkin and Howard in their volume *The Emerging Order* make this assessment: "Of one thing there is little doubt, the evangelical community is amassing a base of potential power that dwarfs every other competing interest in American society today. A close look at the evangelical communications network and infrastructure should convince even the skeptic that it is now the single most important cultural force in American life." And listen to this, if you please: "Today, 1300 radio stations—one out of every seven in America is Christian owned and operated." . . . Many of those who populate this religious position want prayer in schools but don't seem to mind too much if low tax rates wreck the school system. Yes, they want prayer in schools even if the schools are inadequate and segregated. They want to protect the home by not having sex education in the schools. It is all very confusing—those who have experienced the presence of Christ preparing a political hit list and bragging about it. While we and the constituency that we represent have media experts without any real impact on the media. The TV waves belong to those who push emotional highs and sometimes omit the cognitive aspect of religion. They have their own record industry, their own publishing houses, and we keep running around in circles. We have been frightened witlessly into becoming a non-positioned American institution. We sit around with our hands behind our backs with mouths slammed shut on the issues while we dare to wonder if we should work together. Why the handwriting is on the wall. Let's get serious, and fall in love. . . .

It is quite possible that praying and thinking together we might turn tragedy into triumph, crisis into accomplishment and radicalism into reform. In our efforts to coalesce into a majority, I think that we must confess we have at times been too one-sided and lost sight of essence. The emotional experience must be tied in with the ethical in society. We are for Born Again Christians—this is the heart of the Gospel. Man is born again into a community to serve and witness, not for personal kicks. If we work together I think that we can demythologize some of the stereotypes that threaten us and our society. . . .

> The responsibility for change therefore lies within us. We must begin with ourselves, teaching ourselves not to close our minds prematurely to the novel, the surprising or the seemingly radical. This means fighting off the idea assassin who rushes forward to kill any new suggestion on grounds of its impracticality, while defending whatever now exists as practical, no matter how absurd, oppressive or unworkable it might be. It means fighting for the freedom of expression, the right of people to voice their ideas, even if heretical. We have a destiny to create.*

We have a heritage—the heritage of John Wesley who preached not so much from enthroned pulpits but in the fields to the miners and laborers. I have a heritage—the blood of Henry McNeal Turner who was a real burner, who in the last century declared that because

*Alvin Toffler, *The Third Wave,* (New York: William Morrow & Co., 1980), p. 459.

of injustice the American flag was a rag—the stars stood for whites and the stripes for blacks. I have a heritage—I am a son of the Social Gospel of Rauschenbush. Have we lost the fire? I have a heritage—I am a brother to Martin Luther King and his doctrine of love force. Will we dare to let it fizzle? Let's get serious and fall in love with each other. Let's get serious and fall in love with our adversaries—the unemployed youth, the lonely Senior Citizen. Let's get serious and fall in love.

The church at Ephesus (heard these words from Paul): "I know of your powers of endurance. But I hold this against you, that you do not love as you did at first. Remember then how far you have fallen. Repent and live as you did."

Letter, National Baptist Convention, U.S.A., January 15, 1981

In regard to the emergence of the Christian New Right, the National Baptist Convention U.S.A., Inc. has not taken an official position but many of the principles espoused by the Moral Majority coincide with our teaching and doctrine such as: Our belief in God, The Holy Spirit, The Deity of Jesus Christ, The Fall of Man, The Doctrine of Sin, Salvation, Redemption, etc. However, there are wide divergences in our teachings and practices in the areas of social concerns, racism, politics, etc. Although there is no official position taken by the convention in this matter there is a voluntary acceptance on the part of the majority of the black Baptist Churches that our ministry must be prophetic and priestly, evangelical and socially concerned. It seems as though the Moral Majority has taken some of our thunder with respect to the political and moral aspect of our lives, but there seems to be a gap between our teaching and practice in the area of social concern. It is true that the black churches were forced to practice ministering to the whole man as a part of his survival strategy in this country. Thus the black minister was forced to teach all areas of life through his ministry in the church because it was the black church that became the matrix for all of the black man's ambition and aspiration, protection and security in a hostile white society. On the whole black churches of our convention do not subscribe to racism, exploitation, oppression, or discrimination among any elements of mankind. It seems that the Moral Majority only espouses this principle in precepts but their practice negates many of the precepts in this area.

Since the prevailing concerns of the white church in America have had so little to do with the more critical religious needs of black people, it was inevitable that the black church must fulfill this role for black people. It is a common belief among black churches that the prevailing doctrine of the white church is insidiously racist and too often its teachings in areas of social concerns are a slave-making, slave-keeping, ego-destroying doctrine for black people. The black churches had to cut across even denominational lines to do for black people what other churches would not do for them. There is little basis to believe that the Moral Majority will get very far with the black church because the black man will be very reluctant to prioritize the teachings of a group with such a wide gap in practice over his church that brought him through torture chambers of two centuries and sustained him with a gospel that has been proclaimed without a dichotomy of social-religious, soul-body, priestly-prophetic categories.

Very sincerely,
Edward A. Freeman

Statement of Dr. James E. Wood, Southern Baptist Convention

During these high holy days of the Jewish year and on the eve of Yom Kippur, as Christians we gratefully acknowledge our strong bonds of heritage and faith with the Jewish community in general and our Jewish neighbors and friends in particular. While we live in

This statement was written on the day of the press release regarding Dr. Bailey Smith on the prayers of Jews, and read publicly in synagogues and churches of Waco, Texas.

a world which still cannot ignore the long historical conflict between our respective faiths, we are compelled to remember the lesson that religion as such is no guarantor of freedom, justice, and brotherhood. Yet we dare not only recognize but celebrate the commonality of our Christian background and heritage with the Jewish tradition and the Jewish people. Whatever differences there are between Judaism and Christianity, and they must not be denied, Christian faith is nonetheless, to the degree that it is rooted in the Bible, the daughter of Judaism.

As Christians we rejoice over the recovery of the Jewish dimension of our Christian faith on the part of Christian historians and theologians alike. The acknowledgment and affirmation of the Jewishness of Christian faith, although long overdue, is one we regard as extremely significant for the future of Jewish-Christian relations in our own nation and throughout the world. As Christians we are convinced that Christianity cannot be separated from its Jewish roots without doing violence to authentic Christian faith. The very place of Hebrew Scripture in Christian Scripture forever binds Christianity to Judaism and Jewish theology. While we recognize differences between Judaism and Christianity, we affirm the integrity and the identity of the adherents of these historic faiths.

Finally, we reaffirm the resolution adopted by the Southern Baptist Convention in 1972, which reads in part: "Whereas, Baptists share with Jews a heritage of persecution and suffering for conscience's sake . . . , Southern Baptists covenant to work positively to replace all anti-Semitic bias with the Christian attitude and practice of love for Jews, who along with all other persons, are equally beloved of God." We affirm with Professor David Flusser of the Hebrew University of Jerusalem: "There is both human greatness and human weakness in our religions, but there is also the common hope for the Kingdom of God." For two thousand years Jews and Christians have uttered the same prayer: "Thy kingdom come!" Zechariah proclaimed: "The Lord shall be King over all the earth; and that day shall the Lord be One and His Name One" (Zech. 14:9). May the God of peace and love be with our Jewish brothers and sisters throughout Yom Kippur and the coming year. Shalom.

The Family Protection Act, Proposed by Sen. Paul Laxalt

Title I. Education

1. Federal education money is denied states that don't allow prayer in public buildings.

2. Federal money is denied states that don't require parental consent for student enrollment in public school courses about religion.

3. Federal money is denied schools that try to exclude parents from visiting public school classrooms or functions.

4. Federal money is denied schools that require public school teachers to belong to a union.

5. Federal money is denied states that don't permit parental and community review of textbooks prior to their use in public schools.

6. Federal money is denied values clarification or behavior modification courses.

7. Federal money may not buy textbooks or other educational materials that belittle the traditional role of women in society.

8. States are insured the right to determine teacher qualifications, free from the influence of federal regulations.

9. States are insured the exclusive authority to regulate attendance at public schools.

10. Local schools are given back the authority over sex-intermingling in sports and other school activities.

11. Private schools are exempted from National Labor Relations Board jurisdiction.

12. A Family Savings for Education Plan is established: Parents may deposit up to $2,500, tax-exempt, per year, to save for their children's education.

13. Most titles of the Elementary and Secondary Education Act are repealed and replaced with block grants of money to states to use for education as they deem necessary.

From *Conservative Digest*, May/June 1980, vol. 6, no. 5/6. Reprinted with permission.

14. If schools require a parenthood course, parents may arrange for their children to be taught the course by a minister or church on a release-time basis.

15. Parent-run schools are granted tax exemption if they fulfill certain requirements, and are granted accreditation for all purposes of federal education law.

16. Federal courts are denied jurisdiction over the issue of voluntary prayer in public buildings and the issue of state requirements for teacher selection and promotion.

Title II. Welfare

17. A tax credit of $250 is allowed a household which includes a dependent person age 65 or over (Multigenerational Household Incentive).

18. A tax exemption of $1,000 is allowed a household which includes a dependent person age 65 or over.

19. College students may not receive food stamps.

20. A corporation may deduct from taxes its contributions to a joint employee-employer day care facility.

21. The pre-1973 Defense Department requirement that servicemen separated from their families send their dependents an allowance is reinstated.

Title III. First Amendment Guarantees

22. Rights of Religious Institutions. Federal agencies may not regulate religious activities such as church schools, religious homes and other ministries.

23. Rights of Families. Parental rights over the religious and moral upbringing of their children are reinforced.

Title IV. Taxation

24. Contributions by an employed person to a savings account for his nonworking spouse are tax deductible, up to $1,500 per year.

25. The current "marriage tax," which penalizes married couples with two incomes, is eliminated.

26. Expenses incurred in connection with charitable, civil, political or religious volunteer work are given the child care credit.

27. Married couples filing jointly are granted an additional $1,000 tax exemption for the year in which a child is either born or adopted. The exemption increases to $3,000 if the child is adopted and either handicapped, over the age of 3, or biracial.

28. Contributions to an IRA-type retirement account for the taxpayer's parents are deductible, up to $1,500 per year for each parent.

Title V. Domestic Relations

29. Child Abuse. Federal attempts to change state statutes on child abuse are forbidden. Spankings are specifically stated as not constituting abuse. Federal funds for operation of a child abuse program without specific authorization from the state legislature are prohibited.

30. Spouse Abuse. State statutes regarding family relationships are protected from federal interference. Private associations to care for domestic violence victims are encouraged.

31. State statutes regarding juvenile delinquency are protected from federal interference. Tax-exempt status is granted to private associations working on the problem, providing no federal funds are received.

32. Parents must be informed when an unmarried minor receives contraceptive appliances or abortion-related services from a federally supported organization.

33. Legal Services Corporation money may not be used in litigation seeking to compel abortions, assistance or compliance with abortion or funding for abortions.

34. Legal Services money may not be used for school desegregation litigation.

35. Legal Services funds may not be used for divorce litigation.

36. Legal Services funds may not be used for homosexual rights litigation.

37. Federal money is denied any organization that presents homosexuality as an acceptable alternative lifestyle.

38. Discrimination against declared homosexuals may not be considered an "unlawful employment practice."

A Politic Proposal

If you are the Christ,
let's elect you king!
   Plenty in this Roman world
   needs set aright.
With you in charge
our troubles disappear:
   the weak made strong,
   the proud brought low,
   the land restored
   to our control.

Come on, Lord.
We'll join your monarchy
and pay you proper court.
   Just say the word
   and our campaign begins.
With God on our side,
your victory is sure.

What do you mean, Lord:
'that's not your style'?
   If you prefer,
   take over the *world*.
Then you can rule us all.
God would like that, too.

I'm disappointed in you, Lord.
What use is "a kingdom
   not of this world"?
With all your clout,
your heavenly connections,
   you could pull off
   a landslide.

What—me?
  You expect *me*
  to change the world?
I'm sorry, Jesus.
We could have made a great team.

But I've got other prospects anyway.
I know another crowd
  so eager for my help
  they've offered
    thirty pieces
    of silver.

                    Peggy Shriver
                    November, 1980

Notes

The Times, They Are a-Changing

1. *New York Times,* Lonestar advertisement, November 26, 1980.
2. Andrew Kopkind, "America's New Right," *New Times,* September 3, 1977, p. 33.
3. Ibid., p. 22.
4. Richard Viguerie, *The New Right: We're Ready to Lead* (Falls Church, Virginia: The Viguerie Company, 1980), Introduction.
5. Flora Lewis, "The Fundamental Urge," *New York Times,* November 28, 1980, p. A27.
6. Jeffrey Hadden, "Born Again Politics: The Dallas Briefing," *Presbyterian Outlook,* October 20, 1980, vol. 162, no. 38, p. 6.
7. Speech by Donald Fraser, August 7, 1979 to Minnesota Education Association with unnamed quote. Taken from *Teacher's Voice,* March 24, 1980.

Entrance from Stage Right

1. Jim Wallis and Wes Michaelson, "The Plan to Save America," *Sojourners,* April, 1976, vol. 5, no. 4, p. 5.
2. Richard Viguerie, *The New Right,* op. cit., p. 164.
3. "The Pro-Family Movement: A Special Report," *Conservative Digest,* May-June, 1980, vol. 6, no. 5/6.
4. Richard Viguerie, *The New Right,* op. cit., p. 162.
5. Dudley Clendinen, "Christian New Right's Rush to Power," *New York Times,* August 18, 1980, p. B7.
6. "The Pro-Family Movement: A Special Report," *Conservative Digest,* op. cit.
7. Helen J. Mayer et al, "A Tide of Born-Again Politics," *Newsweek,* September 15, 1980, vol. XCVI, no. 11. p. 32.

8. Letter signed by "Policy Committee and Congressional Advisory Committee of Christian Voice," no date.
9. Ibid.
10. Ibid.
11. Ibid.
12. Falwell letter dated August 15, 1980.
13. Undated letter, return address P.O. Box 7082, Pasadena, CA 91101.
14. Undated Letter.
15. Christian Bill of Rights, sent in direct mail October 16, 1980.
16. Helen J. Mayer et al, "A Tide of Born-Again Politics," *Newsweek,* op. cit., p. 32.
17. *U.S. News and World Report,* September 15, 1980.
18. Dudley Clendinen, "Rev. Falwell Inspires Evangelical Vote," *New York Times,* August 20, 1980, p. B22.
19. Jimmy R. Ross, "'Washington for Jesus:' A Call that Never Was," *Messenger,* Church of the Brethren publication, August, 1980.
20. Jeffrey Hadden, "Born Again Politics: The Dallas Briefing," *Presbyterian Outlook,* op. cit.
21. See Appendix, Washington Interreligious Staff council statement.
22. Jimmy R. Ross, "Washington for Jesus: A Call that Never Was," *Messenger,* op. cit.
23. Dick Dabney, "God's Own Network," *Harpers,* August, 1980, vol. 261, no. 1563, p. 51. Copyright © 1980 by Harper's Magazine. All rights reserved. Reprinted by special permission.
24. Edward E. Plowman, "Is Morality All Right?" *Christianity Today,* November 2, 1979, vol. 23, no. 25, p. 80.
25. "Preachers in Politics," *U.S. News and World Report,* September 24, 1979, vol. 87, p. 39.
26. Intercessors for America newsletters.
27. Jeffrey Hadden, "Born Again Politics: The Dallas Briefing," *Presbyterian Outlook,* op. cit., p. 5.
28. Jeffrey Hadden, "Evangelical Influences on America's Future," *Presbyterian Outlook,* October 27, 1980, vol. 162, no. 39, p. 5.
29. Quoted in "Whose Prayer Does God Hear?" *Ecumenical Trends,* Graymoor Ecumenical Institute, vol. 10, no. 1, January, 1981, p. 12.

The Pro-Family Tree

1. "The Pro-Family Movement: A Special Report," Conservative Digest, op. cit.

Right Face

1. David O. Moberg, "Fundamentalists and Evangelicals in Society," *The Evangelicals*, edited by David F. Wells and John D. Woodbridge (Nashville: Abingdon Press, 1975), p. 149.
2. *New York Times*, September 7, 1980.
3. Timothy L. Smith, "Protestants Falwell Does Not Represent," *New York Times*, October 22, 1980.
4. *Church and Society*, November, 1980, vol. 33, no. 10; quotes from several articles in this issue.
5. Reprinted by permission of *Reform Judaism*, published by the Union of American Hebrew Congregations, vol. 9, no. 4, March, 1981.
6. Ibid.
7. "Religious and Political Fundamentalism: The Links Between Alienation and Ideology," vol. I., submitted in partial fulfillment of the requirements for the degree of Doctor of Philosophy (Political Science) in The University of Michigan, 1977.
8. Alan Crawford, *Thunder on the Right* (New York: Pantheon Books, 1980), p. 256.
9. Ibid., p. 293.
10. Thomas J. McIntyre, *The Fear Brokers* (New York: Pilgrim Press, 1980), p. 13.
11. Martin Marty, *Context*, July 15, 1980. Reprinted by permission of Claretian Publications, 221 West Madison, Chicago, Il 60606.
12. Jeffrey Hadden, "Evangelical Influences on America's Future," *Presbyterian Outlook*, op. cit., p. 5.
13. Dick Dabney, "God's Own Network," *Harpers*, op. cit., p. 49.

Welcome!

1. See Appendix, Oklahoma Conference of Churches Statement.
2. See Appendix, "Christian Theological Observations."
3. See Appendix, *The Orthodox Church* editorial.
4. George Chauncey, "The Difference Faith in God Makes," *Presbyterian Survey*, November, 1980, vol. 70, no. 10, p. 7.
5. Letter to the Editor, *New York Times*, October 7, 1980.
6. See Appendix, "The Citizenship Responsibility of Christians."

7. Lester Kinsolving, "Should the Church Be Involved in Politics?" *Washington Weekly,* September 30, 1980, vol. 7, no. 33, p. 4.
8. See Appendix, *National Catholic Reporter* editorial.
9. Jimmy Allen, "Television, Religion and Politics," mimeographed paper, n.d.
10. See Appendix, *Christian Science Monitor* editorial.
11. Robert Zwier and Richard Smith, "Christian Politics and the New Right," *Christian Century,* October 8, 1980, vol. 97, no. 31, pp. 937-941. Copyright 1980 Christian Century Foundation. Reprinted by permission.
12. See Appendix, "A Pastoral Letter from the Bishops."
13. Millicent Steer Foster, "A Call to Quaker Participation," *Quaker Life,* October, 1980, series XXI, no. 9, p. 9.
14. Ibid.

Seeing Our Own in Another's Sins

1. Mainline Clerics Unite in Opposition to the Evangelical Right Wing," *Washington Post,* October 21, 1980, p. A8.
2. See Appendix, "A Pastoral Letter from the Bishops."
3. Martin Marty, *Context,* op. cit.
4. Wilma Kern, article in *Quaker Life,* October, 1980, series XXI, no. 9, p. 19.
5. Robert Zwier and Richard Smith, "Christian Politics and the New Right," *Christian Century,* op. cit.
6. See Appendix, segment of Bishop Frank Madison Reid speech.
7. Donald W. Shriver, "The Temptation of Self-Righteousness," *Christian Century,* October 22, 1980, vol. 97, no. 32, p. 1002. Copyright 1980 The Christian Century Foundation. Reprinted by permission.
8. Helen J. Mayer et. al., "A Tide of Born-Again Politics," *Newsweek,* op. cit., p. 36.
9. Carl T. Rowan, "Evangelicals' Role in Politics No Threat," *South Bend Tribune,* September 28, 1980.
10. See Appendix, *The Orthodox Church* editorial.
11. See Appendix, Mark Hatfield.
12. Martin Marty, *Context,* op. cit.
13. Rabbi Alexander M. Schindler, Report to Board of Union of American Hebrew Congregations, Board of Trustees, November 21, 1980.

14. Richard Neuhaus. Reprinted by permission of *Reform Judaism,* published by The Union of American Hebrew Congregations, vol. 9, no. 4, March, 1981.

Religious Challenges to the Religious Right

1. Donald Dayton, "Distinguishing Good Religion from Bad," *Christian Century,* October 22, 1980, vol. 97, no. 32, p. 1003.
2. Helen J. Mayer et al., "A Tide of Born-Again Politics," *Newsweek,* op. cit., p. 36.
3. Stan Hastey, "New Right Leader Admits TV Preachers Recruited," American Baptist Church news release, October 24, 1980.
4. See Appendix, Bishop Reid speech.
5. Evangelicals for Social Action, "Call to Responsible Christian Action," *Christianity Today,* November 2, 1979, vol. 23, no. 25, pp. 76-77.
6. See Appendix, Mark Hatfield.
7. William F. Fore, "Forms of Self-Deception and Hypocrisy," *Christian Century,* October 22, 1980, vol. 97, no. 32, p. 1004.
8. See Appendix, *National Catholic Reporter* editorial.
9. Rabbi Alexander Schindler, Report to Board, op. cit.
10. United Methodist Communications Report: *The Use of Money in Mission—an Opportunity for Understanding,* October 17, 1980.
11. See Appendix, "Christian Theological Observations."
12. See Appendix, *Christian Science Monitor* editorial.
13. John Danforth, "Propheteering," *Washington Post,* October 19, 1980.
14. Cf. Dave MacPherson's book, *The Incredible Cover-up* (Medford, Oregon, Omega Publications, 1975) which argues for a post-tribulation interpretation.
15. See Appendix, "A Pastoral Letter from the Bishops."
16. Paul Moore, "The Church and True Conservatism," *The Episcopal New Yorker,* November, 1980, p. 1.
17. Robert Zwier and Richard Smith, "Christian Politics and the New Right," *Christian Century,* op. cit.
18. Peggy L. Shriver, "Speaking Truth to Power," *Presbyterian Outlook,* September 1, 1980, vol. 162, no. 31, p. 8.
19. Martin Marty, *Context,* op. cit.

20. Robert McAfee Brown, "Listen, Jerry Falwell!" *Christianity and Crisis,* December 22, 1980, vol. 40, no. 21, p. 364.
21. See Appendix, Mark Hatfield.
22. Martin Marty, "Fundamentalist Politics: An Historian's View," *Church and State,* November, 1980, vol. 33, no. 10, p. 14.
23. Letter to the Editor, *New York Times,* October 28, 1980.
24. Jimmy R. Ross, "'Washington for Jesus': A Call that Never Was." *Messenger,* op. cit.
25. See Appendix, Mark Hatfield.
26. See Appendix, *Christian Science Monitor* editorial.
27. *New York Daily News,* October 23, 1980.
28. See Appendix, Washington Interreligious Staff Council.
29. See Appendix, Tulsa Metropolitan Ministry Statement.
30. Paul Moore, "The Church and True Conservatism," *The Episcopal New Yorker,* op. cit.
31. Rabbi Marc Tanenbaum, "The Religious Issue in the Presidential Campaign," American Jewish Committee paper, June, 1976.
32. News conference statement, October 20, 1976, by Episcopalian Bishop Paul Moore; Fr. Joseph O'Hare, Editor-in-Chief of *America;* Dr. Arnold L. Olson, Evangelical Free Church of America and former President of the National Association of Evangelicals; and Rabbi Marc H. Tanenbaum, National Director, Interreligious Affairs, of the American Jewish Committee. See Appendix.
33. Ibid.
34. Milton Ellerin and Alisa Kesten, "The New Right: A Background Memorandum," American Jewish Committee, October, 1980.
35. Ibid.
36. Marc Tanenbaum, "The Religious Issue in the Presidential Campaign," American Jewish Committee paper, op. cit.
37. Alexander Schindler, Report to Board of Union of American Hebrew Congregations, op. cit.
38. Milton Ellerin and Alisa Kesten, "The New Right: A Background Memorandum." American Jewish Committee, op. cit.
39. Bernard Weinraub, "Liberal Groups Report Surge Since Reagan Election," *New York Times,* December 9, 1980, p. B23.
40. "Smith Comment Stirs Jews and Baptists," *Presbyterian Survey,* November, 1980, vol. 70, no. 10, p. 31.
41. Rabbi Herzel Kranz, "Maryland Rabbi Calls for Jewish-Christian Unity for Moral America's Sake," *Moral Majority Report,* January 19, 1981, vol. 2, no. 1, p. 14.

42. "Smith Comment Stirs Jews and Baptists," *Presbyterian Survey,* op cit.
43. Thomas J. McIntyre, "The Politics of Civility," *Christianity and Crisis,* March 5, 1979, vol. 39, no. 3, p. 48.
44. Thomas J. McIntyre, *Congressional Record,* March 1, 1978, vol. 124, no. 27, p. 2.
45. Mark Hatfield, *Congressional Record,* March 1, 1978, vol. 124, no. 27, p. 5.
46. See Appendix, "Citizenship Responsibilities of Christians."
47. See Appendix, "Christian Theological Observations."
48. See Appendix, Washington Interreligious Staff Council.
49. *Christianity Today,* September 19, 1980, vol. 24, no. 16, p. 10-11.
50. Unpublished sermon.
51. Robert McAfee Brown, "Listen, Jerry Falwell!" *Christianity and Crisis,* op. cit.
52. Ibid., p. 361.
53. *Indiana Church Councilor,* September, 1980, Harold B. Statler, ed.
54. See Appendix, Synod of Mid-South Resolution.
55. See Appendix, Mecklenburg Presbytery Resolution.
56. Donald W. Shriver, "The Temptation of Self-Righteousness," *Christian Century,* op. cit.
57. Union Theological Seminary news release, September 25, 1980, Appendix.
58. Lester Kinsolving, "Should the Church Be Involved in Politics?" *Washington Weekly,* op. cit.
59. See Appendix, *National Catholic Reporter* editorial.
60. Bohdan Hodiak, "Religious-Political Blocs Make Church Leaders Uneasy," *Pittsburgh Post-Gazette.*
61. United Methodist Communications Report: *The Use of Money in Mission—An Opportunity for Understanding,* op. cit.
62. Jimmy Allen, "Television, Religion and Politics," op. cit.
63. Ibid.
64. *Church & State,* November, 1980, vol. 33, no. 10, pp. 4-5.
65. Bohdan Hodiak, "Religious-Political Blocs Make Church Leaders Uneasy," *Pittsburgh Post-Gazette,* op. cit.
66. George Higgins, "The New Right Connection" as quoted in the Maryknoll newsletter, *News Notes.*
67. Kenneth A. Briggs, "Evangelicals Turning to Politics Fear Moral Slide Imperils Nation," *New York Times,* August 19, 1980.

68. Helen J. Mayer et. al., "A Tide of Born-Again Politics," *Newsweek,* op. cit.
69. Lisa Myers, "The Christian Right," *Washington Star,* July 2, 1980, p. A5.
70. Evangelicals for Social Action, "Call to Responsible Christian Actions," *Christianity Today,* November 2, 1979, vol. 23, no. 25, pp. 76-77.
71. See Appendix, Oklahoma Council of Churches Statement.
72. Bill Moyers Journal, television transcript, Campaign Report #3, Show #603, PBS, air date, September 26, 1980. See Appendix.
73. John Danforth, "Propheteering," *Washington Post,* op. cit.
74. See Appendix, *The Orthodox Church* editorial.
75. George Chauncey, "The Difference Faith in God Makes," *Presbyterian Survey,* op. cit.
76. Quoted in *Church & State,* November, 1980, vol. 33, no. 10, p. 5.
77. Robert E. Webber, *The Moral Majority: Right or Wrong?* (Westchester, Ill.: Cornerstone Books, 1981).
78. Martin Marty, *Context,* op. cit.

Right On! What of the Future?

1. James Wall, "The Split on the Right," *Christian Century,* December 10, 1980, vol. 97, no. 40, pp. 1211-12. Copyright 1980 Christian Century Foundation. Reprinted by permission.
2. *Time,* December 8, 1980, vol. 116, no. 23, p. 27.
3. "The Election & The Evangelicals," *Commentary,* March, 1981, vol. 71, no. 3, pp. 25-31.
4. Edward Shils, *The Torment of Secrecy,* (Carbondale, Ill: Southern Illinois University Press. Arcturus Books Paperback Series, 1974).
5. Lester Sumrall, *The End Times,* Summer, 1980.
6. Donald W. Shriver, Jr. and Karl A. Ostrom, *Is There Hope for the City?* (Philadelphia: Westminster Press, 1977).
7. Kenyon C. Burke, "Urban Unrest: An Analytical and Programmatic Statement," unpublished paper, National Council of Churches, May 13, 1980.
8. "Klan Reportedly Giving Secret Military Training," *New York Times,* October 25, 1980.
9. Nathaniel Sheppard, Jr., "Perception Growing Among Blacks that Violent Incidents Are Linked," *New York Times,* November 30, 1980.

10. Rabbi Schindler, Report to Board of Union of American Hebrew Congregations, op. cit.
11. David Wilkinson, "KKK" *Home Missions,* Sept.-Oct., 1980, p. 13.

A Personal Prescriptive Postscript

1. Greg Denier, "A Shift Toward the Right? Or a Failure on the Left?" *Christianity and Crisis,* December 22, 1980, vol. 40, no. 21, pp. 355-360.